Overcoming Pathological Gambling

D0165934

Overcoming Pathological Gambling

Therapist Guide

Robert Ladouceur • Stella Lachance

OXFORD

UNIVERSITY PRESS

2007

OXFORD
UNIVERSITY PRESS

Oxford University Press, Inc., publishes works that further
Oxford University's objective of excellence
in research, scholarship, and education.

Oxford   New York
Auckland   Cape Town   Dar es Salaam   Hong Kong   Karachi
Kuala Lumpur   Madrid   Melbourne   Mexico City   Nairobi
New Delhi   Shanghai   Taipei   Toronto

With offices in
Argentina   Austria   Brazil   Chile   Czech Republic   France   Greece
Guatemala   Hungary   Italy   Japan   Poland   Portugal   Singapore
South Korea   Switzerland   Thailand   Turkey   Ukraine   Vietnam

Published by Oxford University Press, Inc.
198 Madison Avenue, New York, New York 10016

www.oup.com

Oxford is a registered trademark of Oxford University Press

Library of Congress Cataloging-in-Publication Data
Ladouceur, Robert.
Overcoming pathological gambling : therapist guide / Robert
Ladouceur, Stella Lachance.
    p.   cm.—(Treatments that work)
Includes bibliographical references.
ISBN-13 978-0-19-531702-2; 978-0-19-531703-9 (pbk.)
ISBN 0-19-531702-5; 0-19-531703-3 (pbk.)
1. Compulsive gambling—Treatment.   I. Lachance, Stella.
II. Title.   III. Series.
[DNLM: 1. Gambling.   2. Cognitive Therapy—methods.
WM 190 L156o 2007]
RC569.5.G35L33 2007
616.85'84106—dc22   2006017469

9   8   7   6   5   4   3   2   1

Printed in the United States of America
on acid-free paper

About Treatments *ThatWork*™

Stunning developments in healthcare have taken place over the past several years, but many of our widely accepted interventions and strategies in mental health and behavioral medicine have been brought into question by research evidence as not only lacking benefit but perhaps inducing harm. Other strategies have been proven effective using the best current standards of evidence, resulting in broad-based recommendations to make these practices more available to the public. Several recent developments are behind this revolution. First, we have arrived at a much deeper understanding of pathology, both psychological and physical, which has led to the development of new, more precisely targeted interventions. Second, our research methodologies have improved substantially, such that we have reduced threats to internal and external validity, making the outcomes more directly applicable to clinical situations. Third, governments around the world and healthcare systems and policymakers have decided that the quality of care should improve, that it should be evidence-based, and that it is in the public's interest to ensure that this happens (Barlow, 2004; Institute of Medicine, 2001).

Of course, the major stumbling block for clinicians everywhere is the accessibility of newly developed evidence-based psychological interventions. Workshops and books can go only so far in acquainting responsible and conscientious practitioners with the latest behavioral healthcare practices and their applicability to individual patients. This new series, Treatments *ThatWork*, is devoted to communicating these exciting new interventions to clinicians on the front lines of practice.

The manuals and workbooks in this series contain step-by-step detailed procedures for assessing and treating specific problems and diagnoses. But this series also goes beyond the books and manuals by providing ancillary materials that will approximate the supervisory process in assisting practitioners in the implementation of these procedures in their practice.

In our emerging healthcare system, the growing consensus is that evidence-based practice offers the most responsible course of action for the mental health professional. All behavioral healthcare clinicians deeply desire to provide the best possible care for their patients. In this series, our aim is to close the dissemination and information gap and make that possible.

This therapist guide and the companion workbook address the treatment of pathological gambling. As the authors note, the considerable increase in opportunities to gamble, particularly across North America, has predictably been associated with increases in problematic or pathological gambling requiring intervention, with prevalence rates currently estimated at 1% to 2% in North America. The fact that effective treatments exist is not well known, and only an estimated 3% of problem gamblers in the United States actually seek treatment. And yet, pathological gambling, which is currently classified as an impulse control disorder, can have devastating effects on occupational advancement and interpersonal and family relationships.

In this groundbreaking program, individuals suffering from this problem are helped to understand the origins and maintenance of their difficulties and to deal more effectively with the consequences of excessive gambling. With a goal of complete abstinence from gambling, a number of clinical trials now exist demonstrating that 80% of participants successfully completing this program no longer present with the characteristics of excessive gambling. Societies around the world would be clearly interested in preventing the development of pathological gambling with its tragic consequences. While that is not yet possible, we now have a brief psychological treatment that works for individuals experiencing this affliction that should be in the armamentarium of every therapist confronting this problem.

David H. Barlow, Editor-in-Chief,
Treatments *That Work*™
Boston, Massachusetts

Contents

Overcoming Pathological Gambling

Chapter 1 | *Introductory Information for Therapists*

Background Information and Purpose of This Program

Changes in gaming legislation have led to a substantial expansion of gambling opportunities in America, Canada, Australia, and Europe and an associated increase in participation in gambling activities. This trend has created a situation in which more and more people develop serious gambling problems for which they need professional help. Lifetime prevalence rates of this disorder vary from 1% to 2% in the United States (Shaffer, Hall, & Vander Bilt, 1997), in different parts of Canada (Ladouceur, 1996; Ladouceur et al., 2005), and in Europe (Beconia, 1996).

This treatment program was developed to help pathological gamblers overcome their problem and effectively deal with the consequences, financial and otherwise, of their excessive gambling. The program comprises a pretreatment assessment and 12 treatment sessions.

Before beginning any intervention that aims to modify a behavior, the therapist must undertake a complete evaluation of different variables, such as the extent of the gambling problem, the repercussions of the excessive gambling habits on the gambler's life (financial, social, psychological, and familial), the presence of other mental disorders and addictions, the risk of suicide, and so forth. The use of questionnaires and of the Diagnostic Interview on Pathological Gambling (DIGP) will allow the therapist to have a global view of the gambler's life situation.

It is also the initial evaluation that will allow the therapist to determine the best way to approach the associated problems. We generally recognize four strategies for treating comorbidity, shown in Table 1.1 (Najavits, 2003).

Table 1.1 Four Strategies for Treating Comorbidity

Integrated Treatment	The same therapist treats all of the identified problems simultaneously.
Parallel Treatment	Two therapists treat the addictions simultaneously.
Sequential Treatment	Problems are treated one after the other.
Individual Treatment	Only one of the problems is treated.

An individual with an alcohol addiction who loses control over his gambling habits only when he drinks may no longer be considered a pathological gambler once the alcohol addiction is resolved. A good initial evaluation will allow the therapist to create a treatment plan that is adapted to the gambler's needs.

Following the initial interview, we will specify the gambler's goal(s) and his or her motivation to stop gambling. This step is important in order to know whether the individual is ready to be invested in the treatment of his or her gambling addiction.

Certain life situations can represent high-risk situations for gamblers. To stop the hemorrhage and help the gambler to regain a certain control over his or her life, the risky situations unique to the gambler will be identified early in treatment and behavioral interventions will be suggested.

In the majority of treatments linked to pathological gambling, a gambling session analysis represents a key step in treatment, since the gambler has the opportunity to express all the ideas that can lead him or her to gamble and keep him or her a slave to gambling. Observing a gambling session allows the therapist to pinpoint the thoughts that render the gambler vulnerable to games of chance. The more the gambler holds erroneous ideas concerning his or her chances of winning or "beating the system," the more he or she is vulnerable to continue gambling. This program will precisely target these types of ideas. Knowing the gambler's erroneous thoughts constitutes the first step of treatment.

As the treatment is specifically designed for games of chance, it is important that the gambler be able to understand the notion of chance. Most pathological gamblers have an erroneous understanding of chance, which feeds their desire to gamble. The definition of chance is primordial because the gambler will refer to this notion often during the course of treatment. In fact, the more gamblers are able to understand the concept of chance and distinguish between games of skill and games of chance, the more they will be able to rid themselves of the illusions created by gambling.

The games are designed in a way to let the gambler believe that it is possible to predict a win. Gamblers who seek the "best" way to obtain the jackpot essentially bet on the idea that they will one day master the game. They will develop a myriad of erroneous ideas regarding these games. Our job is to create doubt within the gambler regarding the veracity of these beliefs. At this step, the target of the intervention is to bring the gambler to recognize the erroneous ideas that inhabit him or her. We will present him or her with information concerning the payout schedule of different games, the independence of events, the illusion of control, superstitions, the desire to chase losses, and so forth. Also, as the treatment progresses, the gambler will come to replace his or her erroneous ideas with appropriate ones, which will help him or her to attain his goal of giving up gambling.

The exercises aiming to modify these thoughts represent the core of the treatment and help to remind gamblers that they are responsible for their own behavior. That is why most of the treatment sessions revolve around these exercises. Through the repetition of each exercise, gamblers learn to understand the thoughts that bring them back to gambling time and time again and rid themselves of the illusory hope of recovering their losses.

It is possible for therapists to personalize this treatment program by adding complementary activities and interventions that they judge pertinent (for example, meeting with the gambler's spouse or inviting the gambler to meet with a general practitioner to discuss problems requiring a medical evaluation or pharmacological treatment).

The posttreatment evaluation allows the therapist to measure the progress made during treatment, as well as the effects of the modification of gambling habits on different spheres of the gambler's life (mood, quality of life, and so forth). The follow-up meetings (ideally for a minimum duration of 1 year) also allow the therapist to monitor the long-term benefits of treatment.

The Problem of Pathological Gambling

Pathological gambling is characterized by a loss of control over gambling, deception about the extent of involvement with gambling, family and job disruption, theft, and chasing losses (American Psychiatric Association, 1994). Despite its high prevalence, this psychiatric disorder often remains untreated. According to a report of the National Gambling Impact Study Commission (1999), 97% of pathological gamblers in the United States fail to seek treatment. And although the history of gambling treatment extends back several decades, there is a surprising lack of reliable knowledge of what constitutes effective treatment for problem gambling. According to a critical review of the literature on the treatment of pathological gambling (Toneatto & Ladouceur, 2003), the interventions falling within the cognitive-behavioral spectrum have the most empirical support at present.

Diagnostic Criteria for Pathological Gambling

The characteristics of and criteria defining pathological gambling are described in the *Diagnostic and Statistical Manual of Mental Disorders* (*DSM-IV-TR*), published by the American Psychiatric Association (APA). Pathological gambling is listed under "Impulse control disorders not elsewhere classified" and is defined as persistent and recurrent maladaptive gambling that interferes with personal, family, or occupational functioning. The 10 criteria established by the APA (APA, 1994) can be used to obtain precious information regarding gambling-related behaviors, as well as the severity of gambling habits. Furthermore, examination of the gambling problem according to these criteria shed light on the consequences of gambling in different spheres of the gambler's life: family, occupational, social, academic, financial, and legal. At least five of the ten criteria listed in Table 1.2 must be met for a diagnosis of pathological gambling.

Development of This Treatment Program and Evidence Base

Cognitive-behavioral therapy for excessive gambling essentially aims to help excessive gamblers understand all the facets of their problem in order to remedy it. The treatment thus helps them not only stop gambling, but

Table 1.2 *DSM* **Diagnostic Criteria for Pathological Gambling**

1. The gambler is preoccupied with gambling (e.g., preoccupied with reliving past gambling experiences, handicapping or planning the next venture, or thinking of ways to get money with which to gamble).
2. The gambler needs to gamble with increasing amounts of money in order to achieve the desired excitement.
3. The gambler has had repeated unsuccessful efforts to control, cut back, or stop gambling.
4. The gambler is restless or irritable when attempting to cut back or stop gambling.
5. The gambler gambles as a way of escaping from problems or of relieving a dysphoric mood (e.g., feelings of helplessness, guilt, anxiety, depression).
6. After losing money gambling, the gambler often returns another day to get even (i.e., "chasing" one's losses).
7. The gambler lies to family members, his therapist, or others to conceal the extent of involvement with gambling.
8. The gambler has committed illegal acts such as forgery, fraud, theft, or embezzlement to finance gambling.
9. The gambler has jeopardized or lost a significant relationship, job, or educational or career opportunity because of gambling.
10. The gambler relies on others to provide money to relieve a desperate financial situation caused by gambling.

also to deal with the many consequences of excessive gambling. Gamblers become aware of their risky thoughts while learning to correct them, and come to better understand the diverse factors that determine their persistence to gamble. Close collaboration between gamblers and their therapists is required, since ready-made solutions that need only be applied are not being offered. On the contrary, by questioning and scrutiny, trial and error, gamblers are guided toward discovering solutions appropriate for them. The exercises carried out during therapy allow gamblers to acquire or develop skills or attitudes they can then apply in daily life. These exercises will also assist gamblers in mastering difficult situations and counter their desire to gamble.

This guide is based on a cognitive-behavioral treatment created, used, and evaluated by our team. Over the past 10 years, we have studied the basic psychology of gambling. The crucial finding was that the majority of gamblers hold erroneous thoughts concerning the outcome of the game. Many believe that they can control the outcome by adopting different strategies. They behave as if gambling can be considered as a game of skills, such as chess or golf! But the main difference between a recreational and a pathological gambler is that the latter is "strongly convinced" that he or she can control the outcomes (Ladouceur, 2004). Therapists need to be familiar with the cognitive and behavioral approach. The treatment, which aims for complete abstinence from gambling, has benefited a number of adults and a few adolescents. Following treatment, 80% of participants no longer present the characteristics of excessive gamblers. Its effectiveness has been proven first by some single-case experimental design studies followed by randomized controlled trials.

First Study (Sylvain, Ladouceur, & Boisvert, 1997)

The first randomized controlled trial combined cognitive and behavioral components. The principal component of the treatment aimed to correct the gambler's erroneous cognitions. Several behavioral interventions, such as problem resolution training and social skills development for difficulties related to the gambling problem, as well as relapse-prevention exercises were added to the treatment. One group of 15 pathological gamblers was treated and 14 others made up a comparison group. Treatment lasted on average 16.7 hours. The results of this first study revealed the following:

1. 86% of the clients who received the treatment and completed it were no longer considered pathological according to the *DSM-III-R* diagnostic criteria.

2. Treated clients, in comparison with the group of untreated gamblers, reported a significantly weaker desire to gamble.

3. Treated clients reported having a significantly greater perception of control over gambling and a significantly greater perception of self-efficacy over gambling during risky situations compared to untreated gamblers.

4. These results were consistent at the 6- and 12-month follow-ups.

Second Study (Ladouceur et al., 2001)

After having observed the efficacy of the cognitive-behavioral treatment, the impact of a cognitive intervention used alone needed to be assessed. Under very strict conditions, a cognitive treatment without any other behavioral intervention was offered to gamblers. A group of 35 pathological gamblers was treated and 29 others made up a comparison group. Treatment lasted on average 11.3 hours. The results of this second study revealed the following:

1. Clients having received the treatment were significantly improved compared to the untreated gamblers on several dimensions: they met fewer diagnostic criteria (according to *DSM-IV*), they showed a weaker desire to gamble, and their perception of control and self-efficacy was significantly greater after treatment.

2. 87.5% of treated clients no longer met the *DSM-IV* diagnostic criteria and therefore were no longer considered pathological gamblers after treatment.

3. The changes observed followed the same tendency at the 6- and 12-month follow-ups.

Although we have always preferred abstinence as a treatment goal in our past clinical studies, we believe that asking people to stop gambling may not respond to the needs of all problem gamblers; if problem gamblers know they will be told to stop gambling as a solution to their problem, they may drop out of treatment programs prematurely or not enter treatment in the first place. But we need to document whether controlled gambling represents an option for pathological gamblers; if it is, what are the predictors for its success? We are conducting a study to determine whether controlled gambling is a viable alternative to abstinence. If the outcomes are positive, we will identify the characteristics of the gamblers who succeeded in maintaining control over their gambling.

The therapy will be directive, almost like taking a course. Each section of the treatment has an agenda that follows specific topics and also involves homework. We consider homework to be an important part of the process. Hence, each session involves a review of the previous week's homework, as well as assignments for the upcoming week. Moreover, the therapy involves a daily self-monitoring of progress.

The following activities are included in each session.

Past Week Review

At the beginning of each session, the therapist collects the self-observation form presented within the preceding chapter and asks about the client's gambling behavior. There are numerous advantages to this task. Given that gamblers tend to underestimate the extent of their gambling problem, this self-monitoring exercise helps gamblers become conscious of their gambling activities, of the intensity of their desire to gamble, and of the substantial sums of money that have been lost. It also helps to describe and better understand the circumstances (or activators) that resulted in gambling, the triggers (emotions, events, and so forth) that caused the person to gamble more money and/or spend more time than intended, and the cognitive distortions that prompted and/or sustained the desire to gamble. Moreover, the exercise enables gamblers to monitor their therapeutic progress. Gamblers can therefore better quantify or objectify the changes taking place throughout therapy.

Review of the Material and Homework

A brief review of the concepts outlined previously is conducted, and the therapist examines the exercises that the gambler has completed over the previous days. If the client has questions or comments about the exercises or readings, the therapist should discuss them. Before going further, the therapist should make sure the client understands the concepts presented earlier.

Explanation of New Material and New Information

During the session, new treatment issues and elements are presented. Using the material provided for each session, the therapist explains the new notions and skills to develop and discusses them with the client.

Homework

At the end of the therapy session, gamblers are told what exercises to complete and which texts to read during the following week.

Steps of the Program

Pretreatment assessment

Treatment (approximately 12 sessions)

Session 1

Motivational enhancement

Sessions 2 and 3

Behavioral interventions:

Chain of behaviors linked to excessive gambling

High-risk situations

Behavioral strategies to adopt

Sessions 4 to 10

Cognitive interventions:

Analysis of a gambling session

Definition of chance

Importance of the inner dialogue

Presentation of the gambling traps

Awareness to erroneous cognitions

Recognition and modification of erroneous cognitions

Sessions 11 and 12

Relapse prevention

Posttreatment assessment

Follow-ups

The client workbook will aid therapists in delivering this intervention. It contains educational materials, worksheets, exercises, and forms for monitoring progress. It is set up in a theme-by-theme format and corresponds with the chapters in the therapist guide. Therapists must keep in mind, however, that it is important to be flexible; there are times where it is in the best interest of the client to answer an immediate need (i.e., crisis due to a major loss), manage the crisis, and then continue the program where it stopped before the crisis.

We have planned the session content so that an optimal amount of information is presented in each session. In our clinical experience, we have found that some clients cannot take in a lot of new material in one session. We have also found that it is important to leave enough time for problem-solving regarding material from previous sessions.

Chapter 2 | *Pretreatment Assessment*

(Corresponds to Chapter 1 of the workbook)

Materials Needed

- Diagnostic Interview on Pathological Gambling (DIGP)

- Gambling-Related Questions

- Perceived Self-Efficacy Questionnaire

- Daily Self-Monitoring Diary

Objectives

- Establish a first contact in a climate favorable to the development of a relationship of trust with the gambler.

- Understand and listen to the gambler in order to know exactly what brings him or her to treatment.

- Take quantitative and qualitative measures of the gambler's gambling habits and of his or her perception of games of chance.

- Evaluate different variables linked directly or indirectly to gambling habits (e.g., repercussions of excessive gambling habits on finances, social and family life, mood, presence of suicidal ideation).

- Measure the gambler's perception of self-efficacy during risky situations as well as his or her perception of control over gambling.

- Assess the presence of other mental disorders and other addictions.

The majority of pathological gamblers who seek treatment do so when their problem has reached a critical stage. At this point, not only have gamblers used up the last of their resources, but they are also struggling with the numerous negative consequences of their excessive gambling. When gamblers agree to consult a professional, it is fairly easy to recognize their problem. However, recognition of a gambling problem is only part of assessment: in addition to diagnosis, many related aspects also deserve examination. A detailed assessment enables the therapist to determine the severity of the gambling problem with regard to frequency and intensity, while taking into account the consequences experienced by the gambler and those around him or her. Furthermore, pretreatment assessment is a necessary step for the therapist to tailor a treatment plan that fits the gambler's specific needs.

This section presents four instruments used to assess gambling activities, which includes the different factors to explore during the assessment of an excessive gambler. We will limit ourselves to aspects specific to gambling. If the therapist feels the need to explore other themes either directly or indirectly associated with excessive gambling (e.g., anxiety, depression, life satisfaction, personality disorders), he or she can easily find publications specializing in these topics elsewhere. Books in the Treatments *ThatWork*™ series that may be helpful include *Managing Social Anxiety, Therapist Guide,* and *Mastery of Your Anxiety and Worry, Second Edition, Therapist Guide.*

The Diagnostic Interview for Pathological Gambling

To cover different aspects related to the history and evolution of the gambling problem, our team has developed a Diagnostic Interview for Pathological Gambling (DIPG). This semistructured interview includes the ten diagnostic criteria of the American Psychiatric Association, as well as subquestions that facilitate the assessment and permit a more detailed account of answers to these criteria. The DIPG also deals with the following topics:

- Motives of consultation

- Games that lead to a partial or complete loss of control

- History of gambling habits

- Information on the current gambling problem

- Consequences of the gambling problem

- Presence of suicidal ideation

- Current living conditions

- Other present or past addictions

- Presence of prior mental health problems

- Personal strengths and resources available

A copy of the DIPG is included in the appendix at the back of this book.

Assessing the Presence of Simultaneous Addictions or Mental Problems

Comorbidity studies have found a strong association between pathological gambling and substance use disorders, particularly alcohol abuse and dependence (Crockford & el-Guebaly, 1998; Smart & Ferris, 1996). In treatment facilities for gamblers, 30% to 70% of patients are reported to have an addiction to one or more substances. Moreover, there is a high prevalence of affective disorders in pathological gamblers seeking treatment (Beaudoin & Cox, 1999; Linden, Pope, & Jonas, 1986; McCormick et al., 1984), with estimates of major depression in these samples ranging from 30% to 76%. Pathological gamblers also have high rates of suicidal ideation and suicide attempt. Studies involving pathological gamblers who seek help have found that 36% to 50% have a history of suicidal ideation, and 12% to 16% have a history of suicide attempts (Lejoyeux et al., 1999; Linden, Pope, & Jonas, 1986).

Obviously, these high percentages are not found in the general population, but rather among a specific population: gamblers who are consulting a professional and who are admitted to a treatment facility.

In fact, therapists who work with pathological gamblers generally expect there to be a significant proportion with more than one problem. Furthermore, the presence of a second problem renders the therapeutic process more difficult for some gamblers. If gamblers show signs of severe mental problems, depression, or suicidal intention, these problems should be treated as priorities. No risks should be taken with a person who is very depressed or suicidal. First, the therapist must ensure that the gambler knows whom to turn to or where to go to if intense suicidal ideas surface. The therapist can also make a life contract with the gambler. Depending on the situation, it might be appropriate to suggest that the gambler consult a doctor and obtain medical or pharmacological monitoring. It is essential to see to the gambler's security. The therapist and gambler can return to therapy once the situation has stabilized.

Gambling-Related Questions

These five questions allow the therapist to quickly obtain a profile of the gambler in regard to the impression that his or her gambling problem is resolved, his or her desire to gamble in the past week, the number of times he or she gambled, the time spent gambling, as well as the amount of money spent gambling during the last week. These questions constitute an excellent baseline measure and allow the therapist to paint a quick and reliable portrait of the gambler at the time he or she fills out the questionnaire.

In addition to allowing an interesting collection of data, these measures are very easy to use. We can therefore come back to them readily during treatment to assess the fluctuations in the client's behavior.

A blank Gambling-Related Questions exercise can be found in the corresponding workbook, and additional copies may be downloaded from the Treatments *That Work*™ Web site at www.oup.com/us/ttw. A sample filled-out exercise is shown in Figure 2.1.

Perceived Self-Efficacy Questionnaire

The client describes the situations that he or she considers the most risky and then estimates the extent to which he or she can resist the urge to gamble in one of these situations. This exercise will allow the therapist

Gambling-Related Questions

For questions 1 and 2, circle the number that corresponds to the way that you have felt over the past week.

Perceived Control

1. To what extent do you feel that your gambling problem is resolved or under control?

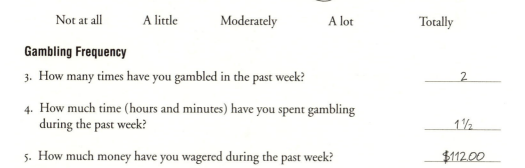

Urge to Gamble

2. To what extent have you felt the urge to gamble in the past week?

Gambling Frequency

3. How many times have you gambled in the past week?   2

4. How much time (hours and minutes) have you spent gambling
   during the past week?   1½

5. How much money have you wagered during the past week? $112.00

Figure 2.1

Example of Completed Gambling-Related Questions

to determine which situations need to be tended to and to create a behavioral intervention plan adapted to the client's needs.

The questionnaire can be found in the corresponding workbook, and additional copies may be downloaded from the Treatments *ThatWork*™ Web site at www.oup.com/us/ttw. A sample filled-out questionnaire is shown in Figure 2.2.

Perceived Self-Efficacy Questionnaire

Please describe your high-risk situations for gambling excessively (for example: "when I am bored and have nothing to do" or "when I just had an argument with my boss"). Then, indicate on a scale of 0 to 10 your level of confidence in controlling your gambling habits if you faced these situations at the present time.

Situation 1

When I feel bored and have nothing to do

If you had to face this situation at the present time, to what extent would you have confidence in controlling your gambling habits?

0-------1-------2-------3-------4-------5-------6-------7-------8-------9-------10

Not at all   A little   Moderately   A lot   Totally

Situation 2

When I just had an argument with my wife

If you had to face this situation at the present time, to what extent would you have confidence in controlling your gambling habits?

0-------1-------2-------3-------4-------5-------6-------7-------8-------9-------10

Not at all   A little   Moderately   A lot   Totally

Situation 3

When I feel my life is a mess

If you had to face this situation at the present time, to what extent would you have confidence in controlling your gambling habits?

0-------1-------2-------3-------4-------5-------6-------7-------8-------9-------10

Not at all   A little   Moderately   A lot   Totally

Figure 2.2
Example of Completed Perceived Self-Efficacy Questionnaire

We find it very useful to ask gamblers to complete a daily observation diary throughout the entire therapeutic process. Gamblers record a certain amount of information regarding their gambling in the Daily Self-Monitoring Diary. The diary can be found in the corresponding workbook, and additional copies may be downloaded from the Treatments *ThatWork*™ Web site at www.oup.com/us/ttw.

There are numerous advantages to completing the diary on a daily basis. Given that gamblers tend to underestimate the extent of their gambling problem, this grid helps them become conscious of their gambling problem, of the intensity of their desire to gamble, and of the substantial sums of money they have lost. Moreover, the grid enables gamblers to monitor their therapeutic progress. Gamblers can therefore better quantify or objectify the changes taking place throughout therapy. The grid can help gamblers realize the extent of their progress when it appears to them that they are no better off after therapy. Finally, this grid provides precious information about the events of the week. Every day, gamblers rate their perception of being in control of their gambling as well as their desire to gamble on a scale from 0 to 100. Gamblers also specify the number of times they gambled during the day, the number of hours spent gambling, and the amount of money lost. Lastly, gamblers are asked to write about the feelings they had throughout the day as well as any context or event that may have provoked their urge to gamble. A sample completed diary is shown in Figure 2.3.

Conclusion

The evaluation of excessive gamblers involves several dimensions. In addition to assigning a diagnosis based on specific criteria, the therapist must obtain information about the history and evolution of the gambling problem, the particular gambling habits of the client, and the client's beliefs and thoughts about gambling. The therapist will also evaluate the presence of other problems, such as alcohol or drug dependence, which may interfere with the gambling problem and its treatment. We have included evaluation instruments available for assessing gamblers. Although

Daily Self-Monitoring Diary

Date:	4/27/06	4/28/06	4/29/06	4/30/06	5/1/06	5/2/06	5/3/06
1. To what extent do I perceive that my gambling problem is under control? 0----10----20----30----40----50----60----70----80----90----100 not at all a little moderately very much completely	50%	30%	10%	0%	30%	50%	60%
2. What is my desire to gamble today? 0----10----20----30----40----50----60----70----80----90----100 nonexistent weak average high very high	60%	80%	90%	100%	30%	0%	0%
3. To what extent do I perceive myself as being able to abstain from gambling? 0----10----20----30----40----50----60----70----80----90----100 not at all a little moderately very much completely	80%	60%	0%	0%	90%	90%	90%
4. Did I gamble today?	NO	NO	YES	YES	NO	NO	NO
5. How much time (hours & minutes) did I spend gambling?	NA	NA	2½ hours	1 hour	NA	NA	NA
6. How much money did I spend on gambling, excluding wins?	NA	NA	$185	$200	NA	NA	NA
7. Specify your state of mind or the particular events of the day.	Very busy; no time to gamble!	Tired, many thoughts about gambling	Feeling tired, depressed and ashamed.	Very sad. Stressed. I lost way more than I can afford.	Stressed. I need to find $250 before the end of the month.	I know that I have to stay away from those machines.	I had a good day at work. I need to stay on track.

Figure 2.3

Example of Completed Daily Self-Monitoring Diary

they are not all necessary for the assessment of excessive gamblers, each is useful for various reasons.

Finally, our experience with gamblers has enabled us to observe that evaluating other elements, such as anxiety or depression, is necessary to develop a proper intervention plan. Any other recourse that is deemed useful, such as speaking with the gambler's family and friends, must be taken in order to better understand gamblers who wish to put an end to their destructive gambling habits.

Motivational Enhancement

Chapter 3 | *Session 1: Motivational Enhancement Session*

(Corresponds to Chapter 2 of the workbook)

Materials Needed

- Exercise: Advantages and Disadvantages

- Exercise: What I Like About Gambling

- Exercise: What I Hate About Gambling

- Exercise: Here Are the Reasons Why I Want to Stop Gambling

- Exercise: Gambling's Place in My Life Today

- Exercise: Gambling's Place in My Life at the End of Treatment

- The Daily Self-Monitoring Diary

Objective

- Clarify the goals the gambler wants to accomplish during treatment and enhance intrinsic motivation to change by exploring and resolving ambivalence.

Outline

- Review pretreatment assessment.

- Use the Daily Self-Monitoring Diary to describe the circumstances in which gambling sessions occurred, the triggers (e.g., emotions, events) that caused the person to gamble more money and spend more time than planned, and the cognitive distortions that prompted the desire/urge to gamble.

Overview

Based on the spirit and techniques of motivational interviewing developed by Miller (1983) and later elaborated by Miller and Rollnick (1991), the goal of this first treatment session is to encourage behavior change by helping clients to explore and resolve ambivalence.

While working with the client to enhance his or her motivation to change, it is important to keep in mind that his or her motivation to change must come from himself or herself; it cannot be imposed. Your task is to identify and mobilize the client's intrinsic values and goals to stimulate a behavior change. Also, direct persuasion is not an effective method for resolving ambivalence. It is tempting to try to be "helpful" by convincing the client of the urgency of the problem and about the benefits of change. It is fairly clear, however, that these tactics generally increase client resistance and diminish the probability of change (Miller, Benefield, & Tonigan, 1993; Miller & Rollnick, 1991). Moreover, the counseling style is generally a quiet and eliciting one. Direct persuasion, aggressive confrontation, and argumentation are the conceptual opposite of motivational interviewing and are explicitly prohibited in this approach. Aggressive strategies, sometimes guided by a desire to "confront client denial," easily slip into pushing clients to make changes for which they are not ready.

Assessment Summary

Explain to the client some of the results of the pretreatment assessment. Accentuate the client's strengths, and explain that stopping gambling should bring an overall improvement in some important areas (e.g., anxiety, depression, and life satisfaction).

To understand the client's motivation to change, discuss the reasons that caused him or her to decide to modify his or her gambling. Is he ready to make efforts to gamble less or to cease gambling? What are the potential problems anticipated? What is his objective for change? Are the reasons personal (internally motivated) or does much or all of the pressure to change come from someone else (externally motivated)? It is also important to discuss the goals the client wants to accomplish during therapy. Even though it has been observed that "some gamblers have the ability to return to and maintain controlled gambling over substantial periods with minimum risk for relapse, it seems prudent to encourage abstinence as the preferred treatment goal until predictor variables are available which could identify the subjects who are able to maintain controlled gambling following treatment" (Blaszczynski & McConaghy, 1993; Blaszczynski et al., 1991).

To enhance the client's motivation to change, complete the Advantages and Disadvantages exercise in the workbook with him or her. A completed example is shown in Figure 3.1. When talking about pros and cons, enumerate concrete facts (money) as well as emotions (self-esteem, culpability) and values (family, honesty). Reinforce the identified advantages of change by probing and rephrasing. Emphasize the negative effects of excessive gambling on the client's life.

Homework

Encourage the client to complete the following exercises from the workbook:

- What I Like About Gambling

- What I Hate About Gambling

- Here Are the Reasons Why I Want to Stop Gambling

- Gambling's Place in My Life Today

- Gambling's Place in My Life at the End of Treatment

Advantages and Disadvantages

POSITIVE ASPECTS OF GAMBLING (the benefits that gambling gives me)	NEGATIVE ASPECTS OF STOPPING GAMBLING (what I lose if I stop gambling)
When I gamble, I disconnect from my everyday problems. It gives me a real high when I win. It's a way to escape when I'm feeling bored. I like gambling; I like games in general.	I lose a "hobby" I like. I'll miss the excitement (the incredible high) that goes with gambling. I'll have to accept that I'll never recover the money I've lost in it. I'll have to face my debts.
NEGATIVE CONSEQUENCES OF GAMBLING (current and potential for the future)	**ADVANTAGES OF STOPPING GAMBLING** (what I gain if I stop gambling)
Current: Financial problems (I'm behind on most of my financial duties). Marital problems (many arguments related to money, lies). Not enough time + money to do things with my family. Neglecting my house (windows need to be changed) + car (exhaust needs to be fixed and tires to be changed). Neglecting myself (need a haircut + a visit to the dentist). Low self-esteem, shame of what I've become. Anxiety, difficulties getting to sleep. Lack of interest in my other activities. Impression I've lost the values I used to respect. Dark thoughts. Potential: Possibility of losing the house Possibility of losing my wife and kids Depression? Suicide? If I do nothing, possibility of losing myself.	More time for me and my family. Eventually, more money for the "real things"; I'll allow myself to have fun and to spend money on things that I have neglected since I gambled (activities with my family, going out to dinner with my wife, little pleasures for myself, caring for the house & car). No more stress related to money loss. I'll stop lying. I won't be ashamed to meet with friends and colleagues. I'll sleep better. I'll regain my true values, I'll rediscover the "real me." I'll put money aside for projects I'd like to achieve (I'd like to buy a camper to go camping with the family before the kids are too old). I'll be more optimistic about the future.

Keep a copy of this page in your wallet or some other convenient place for times when you feel strong urges or temptations to gamble heavily.

Figure 3.1

Example of Completed Advantages and Disadvantages Worksheet

The client should also continue to complete the Daily Self-Monitoring Diary.

Explain that the first three exercises will help the client think more closely about the reasons that cause him or her to gamble in the first place, and why he or she wants to change this behavior.

Next, explain that the forms "Gambling's Place in My Life Today" and "Gambling's Place in My Life at the End of Treatment" will help the client become aware of how much gambling occupies his or her life at present, and allows the setting of a goal for where he or she would like gambling to be at the end of treatment.

Finally, introduce the gambling diary, and ask the client to complete one each day from now to the next session.

Behavioral Interventions

Chapter 4   *Sessions 2 & 3*

(Corresponds to Chapter 3 of the workbook)

Materials Needed

- The Problem Gambling Behavioral Chain

- Exercise: My High-Risk Situations

- Strategies to Help Me Avoid High-Risk Situations

- Exercise: Dealing with my High-Risk Situations

- Five Steps for Problem-Solving (optional)

- Problem-Solving Exercise (optional)

- Daily Self-Monitoring Diary

Objectives

- To help client understand the chain of events that leads to excessive gambling, and the importance of high-risk situations in this chain

- To increase the client's awareness of high-risk situations

- To help client identify concrete strategies that can be used to avoid high-risk situations

- To teach client the five steps to effective problem-solving

Outline

■ Review past week.

■ Use the Daily Self-Monitoring Diary to understand the circumstances under which the client's gambling sessions occurred, including:

- The triggers (e.g., emotions, events) that caused the person to gamble more money and spend more time than planned

- The cognitive distortions that prompted the desire to gamble

■ Review the assignments completed by the client during the past week.

■ Explain the Problem Gambling Behavioral Chain.

■ Identify the client's high-risk situations.

■ Select behavioral strategies.

■ Review the five steps for problem-solving.

Overview

We will now present certain risky situations as well as behavioral interventions that allow the gambler to deal with them. We have divided these risky situations into different categories: exposure to gambling, financial situation, relationship problems, free time, and consuming alcohol or drugs. One section will address the issue of problems in daily life. Finally, we propose a list of strategies that are likely to help the gambler attain the ultimate goal: abstinence from gambling. It goes without saying that without cognitive interventions, these strategies offer only a limited degree of effectiveness. It is for this reason that we use them as a complement to cognitive treatment.

It is first important to reemphasize that it is not risky situations that lead to gambling; rather, it is the erroneous thoughts that those risky situations provoke. The good news is that gamblers can directly act upon these situations as well as work on modifying their thoughts.

Exposure to Gambling

Being in a gambling establishment obviously represents an important risky situation. If gamblers persistently frequent these places, they repeatedly foster their urge to gamble and make it difficult to resist. Given the increasing availability and accessibility of gambling, it is unrealistic to think that one can continually avoid them. However, we know that gamblers can voluntarily bar themselves from gaming establishments. This is certainly the first action to take when gamblers wish to cease gambling.

Certain casinos offer a program that allows gamblers to ban themselves from the establishment. In these self-exclusion programs, the gamblers meet with the establishment's security service and sign a self-exclusion form. Their photo is also taken so that security personnel can identify them if they try to enter the establishment again. The duration of self-exclusions varies according to the gambler's request and the norms in place within the casino. Certain contracts last a few months, while others extend over several years. This measure can be extremely effective: out of fear of being identified and being subjected to the humiliation of expulsion, many gamblers give up going to the casino altogether.

However, certain establishments do not offer this type of program. What can be done in these cases? We can suggest to gamblers that they meet the manager of the establishment where they have the habit of gambling to explain their problem and ask that they be denied access to the location. However, there is no guarantee: certain owners may be willing to assist the gamblers in their process, but others may very well refuse to comply with this request.

Self-exclusion is, without a doubt, the first strategy to use in order to avoid exposure to gambling. Gamblers who reject this step experience ambivalence. They can refuse this option, asserting that control must first and foremost come from themselves or that, if they self-exclude, the only thought that will come to mind upon expiration of the contract would be to hasten toward a gaming establishment. Even if self-exclusion appears to be a drastic solution, it can prove to be a strong tool for gamblers. It becomes a valuable ally, a weapon that protects gamblers until they are in a better position to modify their thoughts.

If it is impossible for gamblers to exclude themselves from certain establishments, they should expect to confront numerous situations that risk exposing them to gambling. Here are some strategies that will help gamblers to deal with these situations.

Finding Oneself Near a Gambling Establishment

Gamblers frequently report that they gamble after work most of the time. Because they generally take the same route home, they have difficulty preventing themselves from stopping at their usual place of gambling. In this case, it would be useful to suggest to gamblers that they:

- Change their routes and ensure that the gambling establishment is not on their way home from work.

- Systematically avoid going to places where it is possible for them to gamble. If despite everything they insist on going to bars, it would be preferable that they go only to those where there are no video lottery terminals.

Other gamblers plan their vacations according to the proximity of casinos or take cruises that have casinos on board. We suggest that these gamblers reconsider their vacation plans and change their destinations.

Finding Oneself in a Gambling Establishment

If gamblers find themselves in a gambling establishment despite their attempts to avoid it, the therapist can then propose that:

■ They remain as far as possible from the video lottery terminals or the counter where lottery tickets are sold. If they remain close to the machines, they risk seeing another gambler cash in an important win or make a substantial loss before leaving the gambling area. The result? Gamblers might think that luck is "in the air" and be tempted to gamble as well, or they might believe that since the other gambler lost, the machine is on the brink of paying out the jackpot.

■ They avoid asking personnel or other clients about the output of video lottery terminals, the results of lottery drawings, or the results of any other form of gambling game.

Finding Oneself Alone in a Gambling Establishment

For certain gamblers, the problem is not so much being in a gambling establishment as it is going alone. In fact, gamblers may regularly go to bars in the company of friends without being tempted to gamble: even if some thoughts about gambling suddenly appear, the presence of their friends occupies them and keeps them away from danger. On the other hand, when gamblers find themselves alone in such an establishment, the likelihood that they will succumb to gambling increases. In this case, the therapist can suggest to gamblers that they never go to gambling places alone. They should leave the establishment with the people who accompanied them, even if they would rather stay a few minutes more to finish their drink. This is because the idea of gambling will surely tempt them as soon as they are alone.

Receiving an Invitation to Gamble

Receiving an invitation to go to a gambling establishment is another risky situation that deserves consideration. Does the gambler find it difficult to refuse these invitations? In this case, the therapist can work with gamblers to:

■ Learn to assert themselves and develop strategies to refuse such offers. In this respect, role-playing contributes to this assertiveness training: during these exercises gamblers learn to say "no," first using the therapist as a model and then playing their own role. Finally, once gamblers have well-integrated ways of rejecting invitations and are able to express their refusal, the therapist can encourage them to apply these skills in their daily interactions with others.

- Discuss their gambling problem with friends and family, and tell them that they are in the process of dealing with this difficulty. Friends and family should be informed that they should avoid inviting the gambler to bars or gambling establishments if they wish to assist the gambler in his or her process. If most of the gambler's friends are linked, closely or not, to his or her gambling activities, it is justifiable to make changes to certain relationships or to question them.

Financial Situation

What is the element that contributes to the persistence of gambling habits? Obviously it is the amount of money available. That fact is undeniable and logical. The more money the gambler has, the more he or she risks gambling it. Consequently, in addition to avoiding exposure to gambling, we suggest that gamblers restrict their access to money as much as possible. Gamblers can temporarily transfer the management of their money to a loved one or a third person, or engage the services of a financial consultant.

Close friends and relatives can help gamblers to better manage their income and spending, particularly for meeting their essential needs (food, lodging, clothing) and paying their debts or other loans. Certain gamblers will find it humiliating to give control of their finances to a close friend or relative. However, other gamblers understand that in the short run, humiliation is better than the risk of losing it all.

The therapist and gambler can also discuss the possibility of requesting the services of a financial consultant or an organization to learn how to establish a budget according to the gambler's revenues and current expenses. The financial consultant and gambler can assess the gambler's financial situation and decide what actions to take. This financial consultant could accompany him or her during various procedures such as declaring bankruptcy or taking steps to consolidate loans. If gamblers settle their financial situation, they will be less preoccupied by the idea of gambling to make money and will be in a better position to undergo therapy.

However, if gamblers cannot resort to one or another of these strategies, the therapist can suggest some simple means that are applicable to certain situations in order to temper the urge to gamble. If gamblers have money on hand, they should carry only a limited amount with them. The therapist can also suggest that they not keep any money at all with them: it could become the pretext to gamble a small amount, which may seem banal or not very serious, with the hopes of making a quick win.

Gamblers who have access to money should consider the following actions:

■ Canceling their credit cards

■ Not carrying an automatic banking machine (ATM) card, which allows the gambler to pay for purchases without manipulating money. In addition to allowing easy withdrawal of money, using an ATM card does not allow the gambler to see the account balance when purchasing something.

■ Limiting access to their bank account by requesting that a cosigner be required for all cash withdrawals

■ Giving clear instructions to friends, family, and owners of gambling establishments that they are not to lend the gambler any money

Gamblers who receive a regular inflow of money (e.g., salaries, wins, gifts) can:

■ Ask that the check be automatically deposited into their bank account, to avoid having any contact with it

■ Be accompanied by a close friend or relative when depositing money into their bank account

■ Give the check to a spouse or a trusted person

- Plan the payday scenario in advance: plan all of the day's activities and each movement in detail

- Warn a friend or relative of the next arrival of money and discuss solutions

- Give another person the responsibility of picking up the mail so as not to be in direct contact with checks received

Lack of money is as risky a situation as access to money. In fact, gamblers with financial difficulties become extremely preoccupied by payments to be made and debts to settle. The result is that while they may first seek real solutions to deal with the problem, they may then say that, in the end, gambling remains the most rapid means of making money, even if they have lost everything. Thus, several risky situations are directly linked to a lack of financial resources. Here are a few:

- Lacking money to pay for rent, food, and clothing

- Receiving a bill

- Having lost the evening before

- Wanting to buy a birthday present for a loved one

- Being invited to an outing or a leisure activity and not having enough money to participate

How can one decrease this financial stress? Simply through communication: gamblers must discuss their gambling problem with friends and family.

Relationship Difficulties

Gamblers often isolate themselves because of their gambling problems, and little by little they abandon friends and family. This distance frequently establishes itself on both sides. If gamblers distance themselves because of their gambling activities and sink into their problem, family members distance themselves through exhaustion and exasperation. Over the course of therapy and during the period of recovery, gamblers learn to live with the consequences of their gambling excesses. In certain cases they can intervene more easily, but in others they must be patient. For some gamblers, returning to their families is not a smooth process. It is even possible that some relationships will have completely broken off and that the climate will never be the same. Why? Because the majority of friends and family no longer trust gamblers: they have lied so often in the past to hide the extent of their gambling problems that friends and family do not know how to distinguish true from false. Trust does not magically return; it is progressively acquired. Gamblers must expect to prove themselves. This difficult situation will often provoke feelings of discouragement, since gamblers are making efforts to cease gambling but obtain little encouragement from most of their friends and family. Friends and family want long-term proof that the gambler can be trusted.

Often, pathological gambling leads to a deterioration of the social network. Sometimes gamblers isolate themselves from others; in other circumstances, friends and family distance themselves either because they have no common interests with the gambler or because they can no longer tolerate the constant requests for money and the delays in repayment of gambling debts. In every case, pathological gambling exacerbates the isolation. Certain relationships will have definitively ended.

By ceasing to gamble, gamblers will face their isolation, and this loneliness constitutes another risky situation. The therapist must warn gamblers of this risk and help them to progressively resume contact with their friends.

Sometimes gamblers have a solitary personality, and the isolation brought about by gambling does not cause a problem for them. However, gamblers may experience the need to establish relationships with others without knowing how. In bars, gamblers are surrounded by people without necessarily being in contact with them. Gambling thus provides them with a sense of community. By ceasing to gamble, they can feel an emptiness or discomfort. The therapist can suggest that the gambler develop a circle of friends or at least begin by establishing one or two relationships. If the client do not know how to develop these new relationships, the therapist could provide social skills training.

Lack of Occupations and Activities

Ceasing to gamble has inevitable repercussions on the gambler's daily life: all of a sudden, he or she has a lot of free time to be occupied. What were the gambler's activities and interests before gambling took up all of his or her time? Did he or she have interests or hobbies? Many gamblers become aware of numerous activities that they neglected or completely abandoned as gambling became increasingly important in their lives. Certain gamblers find it relatively easy to find new pastimes and to resume activities they gave up. Also, keeping themselves active avoids periods of idleness during which gamblers are likely to be flooded with thoughts about gambling. By doing so, gamblers will notice that they manage to find satisfaction by engaging in activities other than gambling that are often less costly and more beneficial.

Other gamblers may be more passive and have always used gambling to fill a void. This emptiness can reflect a lack of relationships, but it can also manifest itself as idleness or a lack of interest in other activities. In this case, with the therapist's assistance, gamblers make a list of activities (new or otherwise) that are accessible and that are likely to interest them. We suggest they find activities they can do alone, as well as activities that require the presence of other people. Certain gamblers seek activities involving a degree of risk or stimulation in order to feel the same adrenaline rushes that were triggered in the past by gambling. In this case, they only need to find activities that adhere to these criteria.

The nature of these alternative, pleasurable activities is of little importance. The important thing at this point is to fill free time in order to discover new interests, while reducing the risk of relapse. Also, part of the money that was lost to gambling will be used to cover expenses for healthier objectives with positive results. Gamblers will perhaps spontaneously choose to resort to such a solution, but they may need assistance with this process if they do not know where to begin.

Consuming Alcohol or Drugs

Consuming alcohol or drugs can greatly reduce the willpower to resist gambling. Since alcohol is often available in gambling venues, most people who gamble do so while drinking alcoholic beverages. It goes without saying that the effects of alcohol can impair gamblers' perceptions and prevent them from becoming aware of the seriousness of beginning or continuing to gamble. All gamblers should be warned of this danger and be encouraged to decrease their consumption of alcohol or drugs.

If the gambler's consumption appears excessive or dependency is a problem, the gambler should be referred to an appropriate resource. Sometimes therapists treat alcohol and gambling problems conjointly, but the therapist must keep in mind that abuse of alcohol or other substances impairs the ability and the hindsight necessary to modify the client's thoughts and behaviors. Treatment in this case can be compared to a sunscreen that loses its effectiveness when the gambler dives into water. Therapy can be very useful, but in combination with alcohol, a large portion of its effectiveness is removed. Gamblers lose their ability to critically evaluate situations. Consequently, while working on the gambling problem, gamblers will first be asked to resolve their drug or alcohol problem. For more information on treating substance use, see *Overcoming Your Alcohol or Drug Problem, Therapist Guide, Second Edition.*

Daily Problems (Frustration, Failure, Rejection)

The lure of monetary gain and the need to escape daily difficulties are two reasons that are often invoked by gamblers to explain their gambling. The desire to gamble in order to win money is largely discussed over the course of cognitive interventions. However, certain gamblers experience difficulties not specific to gambling, and these can incite them to relapse. An inability to deal with daily problems and a lack of problem-solving skills can lead to a desire to escape. Certain gamblers, in fact, prefer to escape difficulties rather than search for solutions. Gambling then becomes a tempting option, as it offers escape and the possibility, as minimal as it is, of winning money. When this chain of events becomes apparent, the therapist must help the gambler find solutions.

The problems that we refer to here can take on diverse forms. They are difficulties or events in our daily lives, from problems at work to situations of conflict at home—any problematic situation that leads to anger, frustration, sadness, or discouragement. From the moment gamblers perceive the advantages of directly intervening in some of these difficul-

Table 4.1 Five Steps for Problem-Solving

A. Clearly identify the problem/Stop and think.
B. List different possible solutions.
C. Assess each possibility.
D. Choose a solution.
E. Experiment with the chosen solution.

ties and show the inclination to do so, the therapist can teach the following problem-solving steps (Table 4.1). A more detailed handout on these steps can be found in the workbook.

There are no miracles or perfect solutions to any one problem. However, these steps provide a model to follow and can help gamblers to solve difficulties when they occur. At first, gamblers will need to familiarize themselves with this way of proceeding. Later, gamblers will notice that the more they repeat the same steps, the less time the problem-solving process will take. These steps will allow them to stop and think about their situation and to make good decisions.

Finally, here is a list of ways that can help gamblers attain or maintain abstinence from gambling:

- Participate in self-help groups like Gamblers Anonymous (GA). Meeting with other individuals who experience the same problem and sharing with them can help gamblers to cease gambling or maintain abstinence. Gamblers will find some support and encouragement among people who have experienced the same difficulties. There are many GA groups. Since these are group meetings, certain gamblers may not feel at ease in a particular group. We suggest that they visit a few groups before concluding that this type of resource is not for them. This type of mutual support truly might not be suitable for some gamblers (e.g., those who are not at ease in groups or who do not adhere to the GA philosophy). Nonetheless, this resource can be very helpful for many gamblers.

- Keep a photo of somebody they love with them and look at it when the urge to gamble occurs. The photograph is not to be used to bring luck, but rather to break the desire to gamble out of respect and love for this person.

- Plan activities in advance so as not to be surprised by the urge to gamble.

- Avoid free time by efficiently managing their use of time.

- Try new and stimulating activities.

- Return to activities they enjoyed before taking up gambling.

- Spend money on other leisure activities.

- Identify concrete goals (short-, mid-, and long-term goals) that they wish to attain.

- Write a motivating sentence on a small card (e.g., "Take care of you." "Do not gamble." "Gambling can only cause problems." "My choice is happiness within my family."

In conclusion, there are many spheres in which to behaviorally intervene, and the proposed strategies are numerous. Behavioral strategies, used in conjunction with the correction of erroneous thoughts with regard to gambling, increase the effectiveness of the intervention and allow the gambler to attain and maintain abstinence from gambling. These two approaches effectively complement one another and address gambling problems from the maximum number of possible angles.

Description of the Problem Gambling Behavioral Chain

Describe the Behavioral Chain for Problem Gambling to the client (Fig. 4.1). This discussion should help the client understand gambling problems on both cognitive and behavioral levels.

A **high-risk situation** is the first step in the chain that leads to heavy gambling. Strong desires or urges to gamble usually appear in specific contexts (situations or circumstances) that *activate* the desire to gamble. These are referred to as high-risk situations. Activation occurs in the form of a thought (or set of thoughts) that provokes the urge to gamble. Once the desire or urge is established, it is maintained and enhanced by other cognitions about the nature of gambling.

After the urge to gamble is established, the next step in the behavioral chain is **exposure to gambling**. The person may contact a friend to go for a drive and, when in the car, "end up" going by a slots venue. The

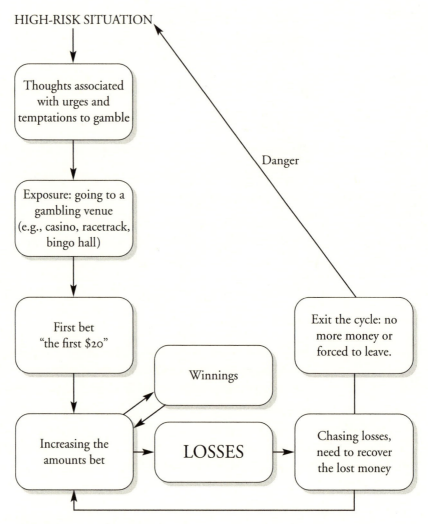

HIGH-RISK SITUATION

Thoughts associated with urges and temptations to gamble

Danger

Exposure: going to a gambling venue (e.g., casino, racetrack, bingo hall)

First bet "the first $20"

Exit the cycle: no more money or forced to leave.

Winnings

Increasing the amounts bet

LOSSES

Chasing losses, need to recover the lost money

Figure 4.1
Problem Gambling Behavioral Chain

proximity of a gambling opportunity is sufficient for a snap decision to stop for a few minutes and, of course, results in exposure to gambling.

Next comes the **onset of betting** and, of particular interest, betting a significant amount of money. In general, clients say they start gambling with small amounts of money, often to "test the game," but quickly increase the amounts wagered.

At this point, clients will experience either an **occasional win or a series of losses**. Either way, the next step is an escalation in expenditures: the first bet for the problem gambler almost inevitably starts a process that leads to higher expenditures. Even if clients win on occasion, the house edge (or the "negative expected win") dictates that they will end up losing, especially if they gamble regularly.

While gambling, problem gamblers often entertain other **thoughts or beliefs** that fuel the desire to continue gambling but are in fact erroneous. Examples include, "I will change tables because this dealer isn't bringing me luck"; "Even though I've only won a small amount, I feel like the machine is starting to pay out. I must keep at it."

The last two steps in the behavioral chain involve **chasing losses** (i.e., trying to recover lost money) and stopping gambling for periods. The desire to recover losses is central in the maintenance/exacerbation of problem gambling because it always brings clients back to gambling and invariably increases financial losses. Problem gamblers become trapped in a vicious circle trying to recover losses but getting ever deeper into financial difficulty.

At this point, the financial problems themselves activate more gambling. Usually, during and after chasing episodes, most of which are unpleasant, problem gamblers adopt a **new set of high-risk thoughts**: "If I could only have one big win, I would quit gambling." "This bad luck is my own fault; I should have never changed my strategy." Eventually, such thoughts tend to include some form of self-recrimination: "I'm so upset that I lost control. I should be able to control myself like everyone else."

Such thoughts temporarily interrupt the **vicious circle**. At some point, however, various pressures reestablish the allure of gambling: lack of money, for example, or the need to meet an external obligation. Periods of inactivity may follow, but regardless of how long they are, problem gamblers still retain their fundamental vulnerability, as often demonstrated when the next high-risk situation occurs.

High-Risk Situations

Use the workbook exercise "My High-Risk Situations" to point out personal high-risk situations to the client. Ask the client to go into detail regarding these situations (e.g., when do they occur, is there a particular day of the week). Emphasize the idea that it is not the risky situations that directly lead to gambling; rather, it is the erroneous thoughts that those risky situations provoke. The good news is that gamblers can act upon these situations as well as work on modifying their thoughts.

Behavioral Strategies

Review the "Strategies to Help Me Avoid High-Risk Situations" from the workbook and identify those that the client feels will be effective and comfortable to use. Using the exercise "Dealing with My High-Risk Situations," work with the client to identify strategies that deal effectively with his or her principal high-risk situations.

Five Steps for Problem-Solving

If some of the client's high-risk situations are due to a lack of problem-solving skills, go over the "Five Steps for Problem-Solving" exercise in the workbook. If some of the client's high-risk situations stem from a lack of communication skills, consider using rehearsal or role-playing techniques to demonstrate skills that are more effective.

Homework

Encourage the client to complete the following exercises from the workbook:

✎ The Problem Gambling Behavioral Chain

✎ My High-Risk Situations

✎ Strategies to Help Me Avoid High-Risk Situations

✎ Dealing with my High-Risk Situations

✎ Five Steps for Problem-Solving (optional)

The client should continue to complete the Daily Self-Monitoring Diary.

Cognitive Interventions

Chapter 5 | *Session 4*

(Corresponds to Chapter 4 of the workbook)

Materials Needed

- Daily Self-Monitoring Diary

Objective

- Identify the erroneous thoughts that the gambler entertained before, during, and after a recent gambling session

Outline

- Review past week.

- Use the Daily Self-Monitoring Diary to describe the circumstances in which gambling sessions occurred, the triggers (e.g., emotions, events) that caused the person to gamble more money and spend more time than planned, and the cognitive distortions that prompted the desire/urge to gamble.

- Go over the assignments completed by the client during the week.

- Analyze a gambling session.

Overview

For excessive gambling, observing the problem is the most important step in the majority of treatments. Thus, during assessment, we induce gamblers to express the thoughts that crossed their mind before, during, and after a recent gambling session. What we call observation of a gaming session is a pivotal step in treatment, since gamblers have the occasion to express all the ideas that incite them to gamble and that keep them captivated by gambling activities. For example, we ask them about their thoughts concerning their ability to outsmart chance; we examine to what extent they feel sure of winning, if they attempt to use strategies to win, whether they entertain any superstitions, or whether they attribute credibility to premonitions. We want gamblers to speak to us about their personal way of approaching gambling games, without challenging their ideas or behaviors.

Observation of a gambling session can reveal the thoughts that make gamblers vulnerable to gambling. To the same extent that a gambler entertains false ideas concerning his or her chances of winning or ability to thwart "the system," it can be said that he or she possesses erroneous beliefs. The treatment gamblers are preparing to undergo will attack these particular types of ideas. Being well aware of gamblers' erroneous ideas thus constitutes the first step of this treatment.

Analyze a Gambling Session

Observation of a gambling session reveals the erroneous thoughts that gamblers entertain before, during, and after a gambling session. The more we know about gamblers' erroneous thoughts, the more we can help to question them when they complete the related exercises. The gambler's last gambling session is an easy session to observe since it is, most of the time, still fresh in his or her mind. The therapist attempts to uncover the context, situation, or element that created the desire to gamble within him or her as well as the thoughts that led him or her to act upon this urge. During this retrospective account, the therapist attempts to discover the gambler's erroneous thoughts related to the conviction of winning and the tendency to predict wins. Furthermore, at this stage, the therapist works at getting the client to speak without restraint. A nonjudgmental attitude regarding the gambler's erroneous thoughts is, without a doubt, the best way to obtain the client's collaboration.

Before starting this exercise, advise the client that you will be asking many questions, so that he or she does not feel "under interrogation."

Explain that this exercise is important in understanding his or her gambling style and will permit a tailored response.

To facilitate the discovery of erroneous ideas, gamblers imagine their last gambling session and the therapist questions them about it, starting with what gave them the desire to gamble. Gamblers then reconstruct the inner dialogue that transpired from the moment the first thought related to gambling was triggered to the moment when they returned home from their gambling session. For example, a gambler may recall what he told himself when he unexpectedly received a certain sum of money. Did he say to himself that this sum would allow him to bet only $20 and that he would be able to keep to this amount? Did he say to himself that it wouldn't be so bad if he lost the money since he was not expecting it? Here, the ways of perceiving the initial event are limitless, but they already provide some indication of the way the gambler thinks. Then, what does the gambler do, what does the gambler say, and why?

The therapist systematically asks questions about all of the gambler's actions and all the thoughts he had. How does he choose where he gambles? Why does he choose that place over another? Does the gambler have a preferred location or a favorite game? Does he have favorite numbers, certain habits, or a particular ritual when he gambles? Does he have a personal way of betting? Does he use any strategies? If so, what are they? How does he determine whether he will increase, decrease, or maintain his bets? Does he have any clues that indicate when to bet? Does he believe he can recoup his losses? Does he think he will eventually be able to outplay the game? After having won or lost a sum of money, what does he tell himself? Does the gambler keep statistics on past gambling sessions?

While searching for erroneous thoughts, the therapist assesses to what extent the gambler is confident of winning and at what point this confidence appears. Is he confident from the moment the initial event that leads him to gamble appears? Does it manifest itself over the course of the gambling session? Moreover, does the gambler attribute certain credibility to intuitions or have any superstitions?

The therapist should take detailed notes of this information because he or she will refer to them in subsequent sessions. Determining the specific "style" of the client (as defined by high-risk situations, triggers to gamble, cognitive distortions, and so forth) will allow the therapist to tailor the intervention to the client.

Analysis of a Gambling Session

Clinical Tip

To encourage and maintain client verbalization, we use a "think aloud" approach. This consists of asking the client to express without reservation or censorship all of the intentions, assumptions, images, feelings, and thoughts that come to mind. The therapist's role is to strike a balance between curiosity and naivety to facilitate a clear and detailed account from the client.

Encourage the client to talk about the context, the places, the people, the events, or any other element that has a close or more distant relationship to the gambling session being discussing. Encourage details about the client's decisions, actions, and any events that occurred while gambling. Ask the client to talk about amounts wagered, to describe or explain changes in his betting style or strategy, the different choices made, and decisions made regarding the game. Question the client on his reactions following a win or a loss. Finally, focus on what happened after the gambling session, and ask the client to express what he felt at the end of the gambling session and in the hours that followed.

The following questions can be used with a slot machine player. These questions can be adapted to other gambling activities (e.g., lottery, bingo, horse races, blackjack):

- When was the last time you gambled on the slots?

- What was the high-risk situation?

- What were your high-risk thoughts (those that triggered the desire or urge to gamble)?

- How were you feeling before you started to gamble?

- Where did you go to gamble? Why did you choose that particular place? What are your preferred places to gamble? Why do you prefer these places?

- How did you choose your machine? Did you ask anyone for information before choosing a machine? If yes, what type of information were you looking for?

- Did you observe other gamblers before playing? If yes, what were you looking for?

- Do you do anything immediately before gambling? Do you have any particular thoughts, rituals, or ways of doing things (e.g., superstitions)?

- Which games did you play?

- What are your favorite games? Why do you prefer these games?

- How much money did you put in the machine to start playing?

- Do you talk to other players before gambling or while playing? If yes, what do you talk about?

- Do you have tricks or techniques that you use to play better? (Do you let the machine "rest"? If yes, why?)

- How do you bet? Do you vary your bets in any way during the game?

- How much of a win is significant for you? What do you do when you win a significant amount? Do you change machines? Do you cash in your credits? What do you say to yourself?

- Have you ever had a feeling that you were going to win? Did you see or feels signs before winning? If so, what were they?

- What do you do when you have been losing for a long time? Do you change machines? What do you say to yourself?

Once the observation of a gambling session is completed, take notes on the high-risk situations, the high-risk thoughts, and the erroneous thoughts of the participant.

✎ Have the client continue applying strategies to avoid/manage high-risk situations.

✎ If needed, have the client continue practicing problem-solving skills.

The client should also continue to complete the Daily Self-Monitoring Diary.

Chapter 6 *Sessions 5–7*

(Corresponds to chapter 5 of the workbook)

Materials Needed

- Reading: What Is Chance?
- Reading: Distinction Between Games of Chance and Games of Skill
- Reading: The Importance of Our Thoughts and Perceptions
- Exercise: ABCD Exercise—Your Turn
- Reading: The Gambling Traps
- Exercise: My Own Traps

Objectives

- Define the concept of chance with the client.
- Establish the difference between games of chance and games of skill.
- Help the client become aware of his or her inner dialogue regarding gambling, and explore the influence of this inner dialogue on the client's decisions to gamble.
- Review a range of gambling traps, and assist the client in recognizing erroneous cognitions.

Outline

- Review past week.
- Use the Daily Self-Monitoring Diary to describe the circumstances in which gambling sessions occurred, the triggers (e.g., emotions, events)

that caused the person to gamble more money and spend more time than planned, and the cognitive distortions that prompted the desire/urge to gamble.

- Go over the assignments completed by the client during the week.

- Define "chance."

- Contrast games of chance and games of skill.

- Discuss importance of the inner dialogue.

- Present the gambling traps.

Overview

The next step in treatment consists of making gamblers aware of the concept of chance, as most people who succumb to these games do not know the meaning of the word "chance." In this step of the therapy, the gambler and therapist work together to establish an accurate definition of "chance." This is because gamblers' errors in thinking are most often based on inaccurate knowledge or a misunderstanding of the concept. As rapid as the process is, it is a decisive step in treatment, since the gambler will be invited to revisit this definition throughout therapy.

Next, the therapist verifies whether the gambler confuses games of skill and games of chance. In a game of skill, gamblers can improve their technique and modify results in their favor. For example, the more they play pool, the better they become and the more they increase their chances of winning against opponents. Conversely, with games of chance, it is impossible for somebody to improve enough to change the result. If it were otherwise, we would have to acknowledge that we could somehow act to affect chance. This does not respect the definition of chance as an unforeseeable event. Accordingly, gamblers cannot improve on chance or master it. We are all equally powerless before chance, and absolutely nothing can alter this implacable law.

Once gamblers understand the difference between chance and skill, the therapist prepares them to work on their thoughts. Because the objective of therapy is to allow gamblers to recognize and modify the erroneous thoughts that incite them to return to gambling, gamblers are informed of the crucial relationship between their thoughts, beliefs, knowledge, and perceptions and the decision to gamble or not to gamble. It highlights the cause-and-effect relation that unites thoughts and behavior. When gamblers realize that risky situations generate the thoughts that underlie their decision to gamble, they can then train themselves to recognize those thoughts whenever they find themselves in a risky situation.

The reading "Gambling Traps" found in the workbook helps gamblers identify their own erroneous ideas about gambling in general, as well as within particular gambling sessions. They learn, supported by the precious help of the therapist, about the various pitfalls of gambling.

Gamblers understand, via the Problem Gambling Behavioral Chain from Chapter 4, that erroneous ideas are present before, during, and after a gambling session, and they become stronger farther down the chain. The more the gambler ventures into the links of this chain, the more it is difficult for him or her to stop gambling without leaving all his or her money behind. This is why it is important for gamblers to be well informed of the fact that risky situations, which trigger the desire to gamble, provide the best opportunity to identify and modify their erroneous thoughts. Gamblers who find themselves in a risky situation and who recognize the thoughts that drive them to gamble at the time considerably increase their chances of making the decision to abstain from gambling.

Many studies have shown that most problem gamblers have an erroneous understanding of chance, and this in turns fuels their desires/urges to gamble. Also, gambling-related cognitive distortions are often based on incorrect knowledge about the nature of chance. For these reasons, it is important to clarify the definition of chance; this is a critical step because the client will refer back to it in subsequent sessions.

Games of Skill Versus Games of Chance

Once the concept of chance has been clarified, establish the distinction between games of skill and games of chance. This step is clinically significant because problem gamblers tend to integrate the "illusion of control" into their gambling practices. They implicitly confound games of chance and games of skill, a fundamental error that reflects their lack of knowledge. By examining the characteristics of each type of game and establishing a clear distinction between them, the client will begin the process of recognizing the erroneous thoughts that cause him or her to gamble heavily.

Inner Dialogue

To set the stage for discussing the client's inner dialogue regarding gambling, explain that because it is not always possible to avoid high-risk situations, he or she must learn how to deal with such situations that are unavoidable and unpredictable. Indicate that focusing on the thoughts or "inner dialogue" the client has during high-risk situations is the first step in developing new skills needed to effectively manage them.

Introduce the ABCD model to the client. Completed examples are shown in Figures 6.1 and 6.2. Blank exercises can be found in the corresponding workbook and downloaded from the Treatments *That Work*™ Web site at www.oup.com/us/ttw.

A High-Risk Situation	B Automatic Thought That Leads to Gambling More Than I Planned	C Behavior	D Consequence
I get my paycheck	I tell myself I can gamble a small part of this money and come out ahead.	I gamble more and spend more than I planned to. I end up losing much more than I can afford.	I feel upset and guilty. I don't have enough money and will have to do without for the rest of the week.

What is the trap? <u>Thinking gambling can help me come out ahead.</u>

Figure 6.1
Example of Completed ABCD Exercise #1: Recognizing How Thoughts Influence Behavior

A	B	C	D
High-Risk Situation	**Automatic Thought That Leads to Gambling More Than I Planned**	**Behavior**	**Consequence**
I just lost $20 at a slot machine.	I tell myself the machine will soon pay out because it hasn't for such a long time.	I continue to gamble, and put in more money than planned. I lose it all.	I feel upset and guilty. I don't have enough money and will have to do without for the rest of the week.

What is the trap? _Thinking that the machine will soon pay out._

Figure 6.2

Example of Completed ABCD Exercise #2: Recognizing How Thoughts Influence Behavior

Explain that (A) high-risk situations generate (B) thoughts that lay the foundations for (C) behavior in the form of gambling. This behavior, should it involve spending more time or money than planned, will result in one or more (D) consequences. Note that consequences can be either positive or negative, and that it is the negative ones that the client is trying to eliminate by stopping or cutting back on gambling. Note also that some consequences are immediate and others are more long term. Positive consequences tend to be more immediate, while negative ones may appear immediately or after a while, and very often extend over the longer term.

At this stage, move your focus to the notion of choice. Through the ABCD exercise entitled "Your Turn" found in the workbook, the client will have recognized some of the thoughts that lie behind choices to gamble when in a high-risk situation. Try to establish that it was the thoughts that precipitated the choice to gamble, that they were a *necessary condition* for the gambling to have occurred. Point out that if these thoughts did not occur, or if they were intercepted, then gambling would not follow.

For this reason, the client needs to develop new skills to more effectively manage these thoughts. Indicate that you will now look more closely at such thoughts as they commonly affect problem gamblers, and that you are referring to them as "gambling traps."

Gambling Traps

Invite the client to read the text on gambling traps in the workbook, and try to recognize the erroneous thoughts associated with each type of gambling that he or she engages in. It is important that the client grasp the significance of these erroneous thoughts—that they are the "enemies" of self-control in relation to gambling. A copy of the reading is provided on pages 62–71.

When the client has finished reading the text, review the content together to make sure that it is well understood. In so doing, take the examples from the text and discuss them with the client. During this session, make links between the points in the text and the erroneous thoughts you noted during the simulated gambling session.

Wherever the opportunity presents itself, refer to the client's previous words and verify whether he or she is expressing a thought that reflects an accurate appreciation of chance, or whether it is an erroneous thought. If it is the latter, help the client to identify what type of erroneous thought it is, and why it is incorrect. The objective is to help the client develop skills for detecting his or her own erroneous thoughts.

Homework

✎ Have client review the "What Is Chance?" and "Distinction Between Games of Chance and Games of Skill" readings from the workbook.

✎ Have client read "The Importance of Our Thoughts and Perceptions."

✎ Instruct client to complete "ABCD Exercise—Your Turn."

✎ Have client read "The Gambling Traps."

✎ Instruct client to complete the "My Own Traps" exercise.

✎ Have client continue applying strategies to avoid/manage high-risk situations.

✎ If needed, have client continue practicing problem-solving skills.

The client should continue to complete the Daily Self-Monitoring Diary.

In the heat of gambling, it is common to feel that your chances of winning are almost certain. You hope to beat the odds and hit the jackpot, and winning is all you are focused on. This is the precise point where emotion takes over from reason and sells you on the idea that your turn to win is about to come. And once this idea takes hold, you continue to bet more and more.

This reading reviews some of the thoughts and ideas that lie behind such emotions. They are usually false and are known as "gambling traps" because they cause you to lose much more than you planned to or can afford.

To begin with, it is important to understand the difference between emotions when you are *not* gambling as opposed to emotions when you *are*.

When you are not gambling, you are emotionally detached and in what is known as a "cold" situation. Your thoughts tend to be more realistic and more accurately reflect how luck or chance can work against you. But when the desire to gamble strikes, you become emotionally aroused and move into a "hot" situation. This is when you are likely to fall into emotional and mental traps, and when you most need to resist thoughts saying that you are likely to win.

By understanding the emotional and mental traps that are part of gambling, you will gain powerful tools to protect yourself from heavy losses.

What Is Chance?

The first step is to understand the true meaning of luck or "chance." Chance is something that you cannot *predict* or *control*. You cannot *foresee* the outcome, and you cannot *control or influence* the outcome.

In games of *skill* (e.g., golf, darts, soccer, or hockey), the results depend very much on the amount of effort and perseverance you invest. And you can improve through practice: the more you practice, the better you become, very often making you better than someone who doesn't practice.

In games of *chance*, it is impossible to develop or improve winning strategies or to influence outcomes. There simply are no skills involved, and so there is no way to improve your skills or make you better than anyone else. Whenever anyone does win, it is only as a result of chance.

Casinos and slots venues *only* offer games of chance (although they may be disguised as games of skill). For example, even though you are allowed to choose your number when playing roulette, it is impossible to control or predict where the ball will stop. This same reality also applies to slot machines: no "ability" is required other than putting in money and pressing the button. You have no control over the outcome, despite design features that give you "choices" and encourage you to believe otherwise.

Why You Can't Improve in Games of Chance

There are two main reasons why gamblers think they can improve their chances of winning. First, they believe that outcomes (winning or losing) are somehow linked to previous results. Second, they believe there are things they can do to improve their odds. The following sections show why both beliefs are completely false, and how they form the basis for gambling problems.

Rule 1: The Independence of Events

All games of chance operate within an absolute law known as the "independence of events." This means that each play is a separate "event" and is in no way influenced by earlier plays or events—that is, it is *independent* of all previous outcomes.

Our first inclination before engaging in any form of gambling is to watch and look for patterns. It is natural to assume that studying something will reveal strategies that can improve our chances of winning. The truth is, however, that observation only lets us see things that are not there: all strategies are completely useless.

The "independence of events" can be understood by imagining a simple experiment. In it, a single red marble is set among a thousand white ones in a bin (much like those in lottery drawings that can be turned by a handle on the side). The task is to close your eyes, select a marble from the bin, and bet on your chances of selecting the red marble. If you select a white marble, you lose. *You then have to put it back into the bin*, which is well stirred by turning the handle a few times, and try again.

Imagine now that you have drawn 50 times in a row, and on each attempt you drew a white marble. Here is a key question: After 50 unsuccessful attempts, are you "due" (or more likely) to pick the red marble on the 51st draw? The answer, of course, is "no."

This type of gambling is known as a *replacement draw*. Every white marble that is drawn is put back into the bucket. Before your first draw, your chances of picking the red marble were 1,000 to 1. When you put the first white marble you drew back in the bin (and stirred it well to mix them all up again), you *reset the game* to 1,000 to 1 odds again. You can see how you always have one chance in a thousand of winning. Even after betting 50, 100, or 300 times, you are no "closer" to selecting the red marble than you were the very first time. And, let's face it, the chances of picking the red marble in 1,000 to 1 odds are pretty slim, as every gambling provider knows.

Applying the Facts

The hard facts are that the number of attempts and your history of losing in no way influence your chances of winning on any try. This is what "independence of events" means.

"What if I draw 1,000 times?" you might ask. "Am I likely to win?" Again, the answer is not what you would hope for. In a replacement draw, the odds are that you would have to draw many more than a thousand times before you are likely to get your first win. Try it with some friends: get a bag and place 19 white marbles and 1 red one in it. Let each person draw, and then put the selected marble back in the bag. Shake it and let someone draw again. Record how many draws are made versus the number of wins in this replacement draw with "fabulous" odds of only 20 to 1! You will be dismayed to learn that 20 to 1 odds in no way means that someone wins every 20 draws.

Now let's apply this information to the slots. As you know, players often vary how quickly they play, the amount they bet, the precise moment they push the button, and so on. The red marble experiment shows us that whether you make 300 draws quickly or slowly, vary the amount you bet on each draw, or close your eyes waiting for an inspired moment to make your draw in no way alters your chances of winning.

The "independence of events" means:

▪ It is impossible to predict (or correctly anticipate) any outcome.

▪ Your chances of winning get no better as you increase your number of bets.

▪ Each play is a completely new game.

▪ The probability of winning always remains the same.

The bottom line is, you *never* "get closer" to winning.

Recognizing Traps

Gambling venues *only* offer games of chance. In so doing, they ensure that the law of independence of outcomes always applies, and you can never improve your performance.

Gambling traps occur when people's thoughts take over and tell them it is somehow possible to improve their chances. Very often, such thoughts lead to betting more money than was planned or could be afforded. They are the paths to *impaired control* and gambling problems.

Here are some direct quotes showing how gamblers overlook the independence of outcomes and fall into traps:

"At roulette, you are in a better position after three even numbers come up in a row. This means that a series of odd numbers are due soon."

"At roulette, I bet the same number all night long. I start by looking at the summary table and choose one that hasn't come up in a long time. Then, I stick with it: each loss means the likelihood of it coming up gets nearer!"

"It is better to find out how a slot machine has done during the day. Playing a machine that hasn't paid out all day is a smart strategy!"

"When the blackjack dealer has been lucky many times in a row, I increase the amount of my bet because he is due to lose."

At the slots, many players believe it's preferable to change machines after five or six plays if it doesn't pay out. Thinking this way suggests two possibilities:

■ The machine keeps track of the bets and past payouts in order to "decide" it's time for the next payout.

■ Wins are determined in advance and put on a "conveyor belt"— each losing play moves the next win one step closer, and winning is just a matter of persevering.

But, as we now know, both "theories" are completely wrong and are traps. Think back to the red marble experiment. The marbles don't keep track of your losses and "decide" they'll push the red one into your hand (possibility 1 above). Nor are slots like gumball machines, where the foil-wrapped winner gets closer to the delivery chute with each loss (possibility 2 above).

With replacement draws, each play is independent of all past ones, and winning is *all about* chance. Also, keep in mind that your chances in any game are so small that you can never count on them.

These facts mean that every dollar spent over your limit is almost a guaranteed loss.

Rule 2: Illusions of Control

A second critical fact in regaining control over your gambling is to recognize that you have no control over chance and nothing you do will increase your chances of winning. Believing you can influence a gambling outcome is known as an "illusion of control." The following sections review common illusions of control for different games.

Slot Machines Illusions

Slot machines are designed to create illusions of control. Although all have similar electronics on the inside, each presents a different "face" to the player. This is where subtle traps are put in to create illusions of control. The designer's skill is reflected in how difficult it is to resist the illusion.

For each play, the slot machine simply draws a random number using an electronic generator, and the outcome is coded as either a win (large or small) or a loss. This means that a random outcome is selected every time you press the play button. By pressing the button, all you do is generate the random number and reveal the outcome.

The amount you wager can alter the size of the "potential" pot but has no impact on the probability of winning. When you choose to press the button has no impact, nor does it serve any purpose to vary the amount you bet hoping this will influence the programming of the machine. Regardless of any actions you take, the probability of winning on any play is the same.

At the slots, it's an illusion to think that you can increase your chances by:

- Observing a machine's cycles or *patterns* of winning or losing

- Choosing a machine by the amount paid out that day, as if there are "full" or "empty" machines

- Choosing a slot machine that just "took another player's money"

- "Testing" the machine with small initial bets

- Pressing the button at a specific moment or betting on a preferred machine

- Changing bets or machines if the machine doesn't pay

- Letting the machine "rest" by changing games

- Pressing the start button in different ways (e.g., changing your level of force, hitting it repeatedly, or changing your speed of betting)

- Cashing in (or not) and believing either action might affect future outcomes

- Betting more heavily when the machine is "starting to pay out"

- Returning to the same machine the next day, having lost the night before

- Calculating in your mind the number of bets made, the time, and so forth

- Observing payouts at nearby machines to decide the amount you bet

- Using *any* trick, strategy, or system

Lottery Illusions

Although relatively inoffensive, lotteries promote a range of illusions of control. Common examples are to think you can increase your chances of winning by:

- Choosing numbers such as birthdays

- Keeping track of winning numbers from previous drawings

- Keeping the same numbers from drawing to drawing

- Betting on lucky numbers

- Placing numbers evenly on the betting form

- Varying where tickets are purchased

- Studying winning patterns of sports teams

Bingo Illusions

At bingo, common illusions are to think you can increase your chances of winning by:

- Choosing cards that have your favorite numbers on them

- Marking numbers in a certain way

- Choosing a table where nobody has won in a while

- Choosing a table where several people have won recently

- Not playing cards with certain numbers on them

- Going to play with someone you consider to be "lucky"

Blackjack Illusions

At blackjack, there is no better strategy than to follow the basic rules known to all players. Any other strategy puts you at a disadvantage in the long run. With this in mind, you really have no decisions to make, and it is an illusion to think you can increase your chances of winning by:

- Trying to memorize or count cards

- Choosing a particular table, seat, or dealer

- Observing the cards dealt to other players in order to decide whether to draw another of your own

- Observing the style of other players before starting to play

- Slowing or speeding up the pace of the game

- Placing very high bets

Roulette Illusions

The arrangement of the numbers inside the roulette wheel can inspire thoughts about control, and introducing the croupier into the equation allows for even more. The rolling of the ball encourages you to observe the croupier's technique in hopes of better predicting the outcome.

At roulette, it is an illusion to think you can increase your chances of winning by:

- Observing the croupier's rolling technique (e.g., rhythm, regularity, continuity)

- Choosing a particular table, seat, or croupier

- Watching previous rolls and keeping count of outcomes

- Betting on "lucky" numbers

- Watching a player who is winning and placing similar bets

- Increasing the size of your bet if the ball stops close to your preferred numbers

Horse Racing Illusions

Research has shown that experienced horse gamblers ("handicappers") achieve the same level of payout as rookies. The bottom line is that, despite studying an impressive amount of statistical information, they lose just as much as someone who selects horses on a random basis. Yet they are considered "specialists," even though their financial situations often turn out to be disastrous.

Horse betters embrace a range of illusions, each implying that chance is a predictable and logical "science." They are convinced that their skills improve with time and study, and that experience plays in their favor. Many such "experts" dream of earning a living within their chosen "science."

When betting on the horses, it is an illusion to think you can increase your chances of winning by:

- Studying statistics from previous races

- Calculating future race times from a horse's previous times

- Playing the "rebound"—a horse that paid out terribly will do better in the next

- Assessing the race distance, the track condition, or type of surface (grass or dirt)

- Analyzing the physical attributes of the horse (e.g., muscularity, way of standing)

Superstitions

Superstitions are ritualistic, magical, or "sacred" thoughts and actions believed to have the power to overcome chance. They tap into gamblers' strong desires to win and mark a transition into mysticism in the effort to predict wins.

Here are quotes for common gambling-related superstitions:

- "The 21st of the month is lucky as it is made up of three times the number seven."

- "I start to win immediately after eating a cheese sandwich. I know it sounds odd, but it works for me."

- "When I don't try to win, I do. Wanting to win undermines my luck and makes me lose. I need to pull back on desire and get into the zone."

In Conclusion

At this point, you can appreciate that if you do not counter erroneous thoughts, particularly when you are emotionally aroused by the desire to gamble (i.e., in a "hot" situation), you are more likely to incur substantial losses.

Failing to control these thoughts allows you to develop a false feeling of personal effectiveness and to believe that all the time and money invested in gambling is bound to be rewarded one day.

By maintaining these false beliefs, you lay the foundations for impaired control, problem gambling, and harm to your health, social, and financial well-being.

Chapter 7   *Sessions 8–10*

(Corresponds to chapter 6 of the workbook)

Materials Needed

▣ Exercise: It's My Call

Objectives

▣ Help the client recognize the erroneous cognitions that affect his or her gambling

▣ Develop skills for challenging and casting doubt on the erroneous thoughts that lead to excessive gambling

▣ Help the client appreciate that he or she has the power to decide to gamble or not

Outline

▣ Review past week.

▣ Use the Daily Self-Monitoring Diary to describe the circumstances in which gambling sessions occurred, the triggers (e.g., emotions, events) that caused the person to gamble more money and spend more time than planned, and the cognitive distortions that prompted the desire/urge to gamble. Go over the assignments completed by the client during the week.

▣ Identify/challenge erroneous cognitions.

Once gamblers understand what errors in thinking are and the consequences these have on decisions, they are then able to undertake exercises that challenge erroneous thoughts. Challenging erroneous thoughts is the essence of the entire therapeutic process. To support their decision to no longer gamble, gamblers work at modifying spontaneous thoughts that incite them to gamble or that encourage them to continue gambling. These practical exercises allow gamblers to organize their thoughts and to act upon them. The more they complete these exercises, the more they become capable of resisting their desire to gamble. In fact, through these exercises, gamblers learn to no longer let themselves be trapped by risky situations and by the erroneous ideas they provoke.

As mentioned previously, an excellent way to help gamblers overcome their urge to gamble consists of bringing them to recognize the relationship between their thoughts and decisions. At the beginning of each therapy session, gamblers relate the occasions where they managed to abstain from gambling despite a strong impulse otherwise. They question themselves about the ideas that allowed them to overcome their desire. Once they have isolated these thoughts, gamblers regularly remember them. The gamblers then attribute a form of mastery over them and are freed from the feelings of powerlessness that paralyzed them for so long. They realize little by little that they have the power to rebel against their desire to gamble.

Erroneous Cognitions

The exercise entitled "It's My Call" in the workbook promotes recognition and integration of the relationship between thoughts and the decision whether to gamble or not. The objective of the exercise is to discover and modify the gambler's spontaneous thoughts, which form the basis of the decision to gamble. With time and training, gamblers become skilled at replacing their old mental reflexes with new thoughts geared toward their personal objective to quit gambling.

Generally, at the time of their therapy sessions, gamblers complete the exercise based on a recent relapse episode or from a prevalent risky situation. The therapist's role consists of guiding the gambler's reflections in a way that recognizes risky situations and the erroneous ideas they trigger. The gambler's task is to identify the thoughts that will help him or her to attain and maintain abstinence.

In this exercise, gamblers take each of their erroneous thoughts and replace them with thoughts that more accurately reflect the realities of gambling and that are in line with their objective of ceasing to gamble. They write down the new ideas in the column representing thoughts that give them control over their desire to gamble. Like when training for a sport, practice and perseverance often represent a gauge of improvement and success. The more the gambler entertains new appropriate thoughts, the less he or she succumbs to the desire to gamble. This is why gamblers will complete as many exercises as there are times when they have felt the urge to gamble or have faced a risky situation. Multiple copies of the exercise may be downloaded from the Treatments *That Work*™ Web site at www.oup.com/us/ttw.

Each meeting begins with an examination of the exercises that the gambler has completed. If he or she has not completed any, the therapist takes advantage of the time to reassess the degree of ambivalence toward treatment. Then, the therapist asks the gambler to do a new exercise based on a risky situation that occurred during the past week. Completing these exercises allows both the gambler and the therapist to remain focused on treatment goals.

What can one do when the gambler's belief seems unshakable? Since the objective of this exercise is the modification of erroneous ideas, the therapist must attempt to cast doubt in the gambler's mind and demonstrate the inexactness of his assertion. For example, is the electric current that the gambler feels an effective way of predicting? Has the gambler previously lost after this sensation had occurred? Has he ever won without having felt this electric current beforehand? To identify these occasions where the gambler's certainty was undermined, the therapist gives him or her as much time as he or she needs to respond. This intervention creates dissonance within the gambler's mind, since most of the time wins and losses are independent of what he or she feels beforehand. In most cases, gamblers recognize the absence of predictive value in the sensation examined and consider modifying their idea.

If the certainty associated with the sensation remains unshakable, the therapist asks the gambler to complete a systematic observation exercise, which aims to compare his or her wins and losses as a function of the feelings experienced before the gambling sessions, should a relapse ensue. This exercise is generally enough to make gamblers realize that their physiologic and emotional sensations in no way assist them in predicting wins. If, contrary to expectations, the gambler persists in saying that the electric current he or she feels is of great predictive value, the therapist then challenges the gambler's "reality" and asks how it is that with such a method of prediction, he experiences so many financial losses. Moreover, why does he not go gambling only when he feels these sensations? Usually this type of question leads to serious doubt concerning the initial idea, and gamblers learn to distrust traps of this kind.

The last part of this exercise permits gamblers to evaluate the erroneous or correct character of their assertions. The cognitive work does not aim to confront; rather, it is presented as a means of recovering control over their behavior. It is hoped gamblers will generalize this way of questioning themselves to other areas of their lives.

Gamblers pursue the exercise by writing down new ideas that help them to master their desire to gamble. They could write, for example, that there is no relationship between their emotions and the machines' returns. Thus, they realize that the notion of "deservingness" has no effect on their chances of winning or that it is even absurd to say that a "full" machine should soon pay out. Gamblers also notice that nothing can help them to predict a win, or that testing a machine is completely pointless since each draw in video lottery is completely independent.

Gamblers finally arrive at an extremely important step in this exercise. They must choose what they will do the next time the risky situation presents itself. In the example we are using, the gambler decides that the next time the risky situation arises, he will invite a friend out to a restaurant.

Though they will be applying cognitive strategies, gamblers retain their freedom to determine their behavior, just as they assume responsibility for the consequences. Gamblers' choices and their freedom to prefer certain behaviors to others are, in fact, points that should be emphasized. Gamblers are responsible for their behavior, and the therapist takes great care to mention this. At this step, it could be beneficial for gamblers to distinguish between pleasure and freedom. Freedom does not involve the ability to continually experience pleasure; this attitude creates more slavery. We need only to think about alcoholics or drug addicts to understand that pleasure in the short run is not a sign of freedom. Rather, it rests on a person's ability to make choices that are good for him or her and to stop making choices that do not respect his or her own values or allow him or her to attain life goals. Freedom also involves being responsible for the consequences of one's choices. By considering the notion of choice and freedom from this particular angle, gamblers understand that the decision to not gamble arises from personal liberty and not an exterior constraint.

It's My Call Exercise

High-Risk Situation	Automatic Thoughts That Lead to Gambling More Than Planned	New Thoughts That Let Me Control My Gambling	Behavior: The Course of Action I Choose	Outcome
I'm at home. I'm alone. My husband is working. I know he won't be back until late.	I could go for a few minutes and try a $20 bet just to check if I'm lucky today.	Let's be honest. I know that if I gamble $20 and I lose it right away, I will continue to put money in the machine, to chase my money back. And if I gamble $20 and win, I will gamble it all.	I'll take advantage of my husband being out to rent a "chick flick." He hates romantic comedies.	I'm so happy with myself. It has been a while since I've done something that enjoyable. I'm glad I decided not to surrender to my initial thought.

Figure 7.1

Example of Completed It's My Call Exercise

Other types of exercises can be carried out to enrich the preceding exercise. For example, when gamblers are able to reevaluate or to reconsider their own thoughts, it is interesting to reverse the therapist and gambler's roles. Gamblers then find themselves in the position of the one who must recognize the erroneous ideas proposed by the real therapist. The activity takes place in exactly the same way as the ABCD exercise—Your Turn. The therapist relates a risky situation, while the gambler systematically questions him or her to discover erroneous thoughts. Using this role-playing game, gamblers experience a powerful mirror effect because they recognize evidence of their erroneous ideas with regard to games of chance. This exercise is simple, amusing, and generally well appreciated by gamblers.

Another simple and efficacious way of reassessing erroneous thoughts consists of recording gamblers' dialogue on an audiotape when they are describing their last relapse. Then the gambler listens to the recording and is invited to detect and correct his or her erroneous thoughts.

Homework

✎ Ask client to complete an "It's My Call" exercise every time he or she experiences the urge to gamble or faces a risky situation.

✎ Have client continue applying strategies to avoid/manage high-risk situations.

✎ If needed, have client continue practicing problem-solving skills.

The client should continue to complete the Daily Self-Monitoring Diary.

Relapse Prevention

Chapter 8   *Sessions 11 &12*

(Corresponds to chapter 7 of the workbook)

Materials Needed

- Exercise: Relapse Prevention: Sophie's Relapse

- Reading: Relapse Warning Signs

- Reading: Emergency Measures Part 1: Preventing a Slip

- Reading: Emergency Measures Part 2: Managing a Slip

- Memory Aid

Objectives

- Help the client to understand relapse as a normal process

- Orient the client to the possibility of a slip or relapse

- Develop strategies that will help to prevent slips or a relapse

- Establish what to do in case of a slip or relapse

- Discuss emergency measures to take in case of slip or relapse

Outline

- Review past week.

- Use the Daily Self-Monitoring Diary to understand the circumstances when gambling occurred, the activators (e.g., emotions, events) that caused the client to exceed his or her limits, and the erroneous cognitions that led to the desire to gamble. Go over the assignments completed by the client over the week.

- Orient the client to the possibility of a slip or relapse.

- Discuss emergency measures.

Understanding Relapse

Once gamblers have attained abstinence from gambling, they face another great challenge: maintaining abstinence. Like addictions to alcohol or drugs, pathological gambling is a chronic relapsing disorder. The prevention of relapse is a crucial and critical element of effective treatment. It is important to remember that relapse is not an automatic sentence to a lifetime of problem gambling for an individual, and although relapse is common with addiction, it is preventable.

The relapse process involves clients experiencing a sense of perceived control and self-efficacy while maintaining changes gained through quitting or moderating their use. The longer the period of successful abstinence or controlled use, the greater the individual's perception of self-efficacy. This continues until an individual experiences a high-risk situation that poses a threat to his or her perceived control, decreases self-efficacy, and eventually increases the probability of relapse.

Relapse does not occur without a reason. There are many contributing factors, as well as warning signs that indicate that an individual may be in danger of returning to excessive gambling. In an analysis of relapse episodes obtained from clients with a variety of addictive behavior problems, Marlatt and Gordon (1985) identified three high-risk situations that were associated with almost 75% of the relapses reported: negative emotional states, interpersonal conflict, and social pressure.

If an individual has an effective coping response to deal with a high-risk situation, the probability of relapse decreases significantly. When a person deals effectively with a high-risk situation, he or she is likely to experience an increased self-efficacy. As the duration of abstinence (or controlled gambling) increases, an individual has the experience of coping effectively with one high-risk situation after another, and the probability of relapse decreases accordingly.

However, what happens if a person has not learned or cannot implement an effective coping response when confronted with a high-risk situation? Failure to master a high-risk situation is likely to decrease self-efficacy and to provide a sense of powerlessness. At this point, a lapse is likely.

Given its many facets, relapse can be defined a number of ways. For some, a relapse means a return to old gambling habits. For others, gambling on only one occasion corresponds to relapse. We define relapse as a return to a gambling cycle or a loss of control in a gambling situation. However, it is important to keep in mind that relapse is an integral part of a normal recovery process.

Relapse prevention needs to be integrated into therapy and addressed throughout the entire therapeutic process. Generally, abstinence is achieved gradually. Consequently, it is essential to discuss the potential of relapse throughout therapy. Gamblers are informed that relapse can even be useful for many people. In fact, rather than perceiving relapse as a catastrophe or failure, gamblers can use it to their advantage by consolidating their gains and identifying the erroneous thoughts that pushed them to gamble again.

In clinical practice, coping skills training (i.e., understanding relapse as a process, identifying and coping effectively with high-risk situations, coping with urges and craving, implementing damage-control procedures during a lapse to minimize its negative consequences, staying engaged in treatment even after a relapse, and learning how to create a more balanced lifestyle) forms the cornerstone of relapse prevention. Some additional, complementary actions that can be integrated into the relapse prevention intervention are as follows:

- Favor a gradual end to therapy. Gradually terminating therapy assures the gambler of assistance in the case of relapse. This strategy also facilitates the gambler's adaptation to the ending of the therapeutic alliance. The process of gradually ending therapy simply involves spacing the last sessions. For example, a therapist can choose to see the client every 2 weeks, then every 3 weeks and finally once per month if necessary. Then, the therapist immediately plans a follow-up. This process provides clients with an anchor, reassures them, and helps to maintain their determination to not gamble, because they know that they will have to tell the therapist what has happened since their last meeting.

- Encourage gamblers to complete their exercises. We know that when gamblers experience a period of relapse, they stop, unfortunately, completing their exercises on the questioning of automatic thoughts. The gamblers are thus asked to use their "It's My Call" exercises each time the desire to gamble presents itself. It serves as a protective tool against their erroneous thoughts.

- Find available resources and evaluate them. This is an exercise that ensures positive results. Gamblers begin by asking themselves: Who can help me? What resources are available in my environment? They then make a list and keep it close by. Thanks to this exercise, gamblers realize that they are not alone and that they can obtain assistance if their desire to gamble is too insistent.

- Promote access to self-help groups. For some gamblers, self-help groups such as Gamblers Anonymous (GA) contribute to the maintenance of abstinence. Within these groups, each gambler is paired with a "sponsor" to whom he or she can turn if relapse is imminent. Moreover, pressure from the group and the solidarity in its members' determination not to gamble can keep some gamblers' momentum in check. There is strength in unity! In fact, all of the resources that are likely to help gamblers should be identified, and the therapist should encourage gamblers to consider them while working on maintaining abstinence.

Possibility of a Slip or Relapse

The relapse prevention theme is implicit throughout the therapy and is consistent with the overall goal of preventing a return to excessive gambling. Once the client has sufficiently developed his or her cognitive and behavioral coping strategies and is ready to end treatment, it is time to introduce the possibility of relapse. Using the workbook exercise "Relapse Prevention: Sophie's Relapse," review the key concepts, including:

- The definition of a slip and relapse

- The significance of a slip or relapse for the client

- The events, thoughts, and circumstances that might cause a slip or relapse

Emergency Measures

Review the readings and exercises in the workbook on how to prevent and manage a slip or relapse, and discuss how the client might personalize these resources to his or her circumstances. At the end of the session, set an appointment for the posttreatment assessment.

Homework

(To be done between sessions 11 and 12)

Instruct client to review the following workbook materials:

- Relapse Prevention: Sophie's Relapse

- Relapse Warning Signs

- Emergency Measures Part 1: Preventing Slip

- Emergency Measures Part 2: Managing a Slip

- Memory Aid

- Have client continue applying strategies to avoid/manage high-risk situations.

- If needed, have client continue practicing problem-solving skills.

The client should continue to complete the Daily Self-Monitoring Diary.

Chapter 9 | *Posttreatment Assessment*

(Corresponds to chapter 8 of the workbook)

Materials Needed

- Section 5 of the Diagnostic Interview for Pathological Gambling (DIPG)—*DSM-IV* Diagnostic Criteria (see Appendix)

- Section 6 of the DIPG—Consequences of the Gambling Problem (see Appendix)

- Gambling-Related Questions from Chapter 2

- Perceived Self-Efficacy Questionnaire from Chapter 2

Objectives

Assess what has been acquired during treatment by:

- Taking quantitative and qualitative measures of the client's gambling habits and of his or her perception of games of chance

- Measuring the client's perception of self-efficacy during risky situations as well as his or her perception of control over gambling

- Evaluating the impact of the modification of gambling habits on different aspects of the client's life

Overview

During posttreatment assessment, the therapist will check whether the client has reached his or her objective. The therapist will also look for *DSM-IV* diagnostic criteria for pathological gambling using Section 5 of the Diagnostic Interview for Pathological Gambling (DIPG) (see Appendix). The therapist will also collect information related to the gambling habits of the client via Section 6 of the DIPG (see Appendix), as well as the Gambling-Related Questions exercise and Perceived Self-Efficacy Questionnaire introduced during the pretreatment assessment.

Outcome Evaluation

The basic question in outcome evaluation is whether, and as the result of treatment exposure, a behavioral change has occurred. This change often refers to a reduction or cessation of the excessive gambling behaviors and consequently to a reduction or fading of the related negative consequences.

The most obvious method that can be used to assess whether individuals demonstrate meaningful improvement in gambling-related problems is the determination of whether clients achieve and can maintain treatment objectives. Another method of measuring progress is to compare the pretest and posttest scores on a number of variables to verify whether there are meaningful intraindividual changes. We suggest you use both of these methods.

Chapter 10 *Follow-Up Assessment*

(Corresponds to chapter 9 of the workbook)

Materials Needed

- Section 5 of the Diagnostic Interview for Pathological Gambling (DIPG)—*DSM-IV* Diagnostic Criteria (see Appendix)

- Section 6 of the DIPG—Consequences of the Gambling Problem (see Appendix)

- Gambling-Related Questions from Chapter 2

- Perceived Self-Efficacy Questionnaire from Chapter 2

Objectives

Assess the maintenance (during the course of time) of progress that was made during treatment by:

- Taking quantitative and qualitative measures of the client's gambling habits and of his or her perception of games of chance

- Measuring the client's perception of self-efficacy in risky situations as well as his or her perception of control over gambling

- Evaluating the midterm impact of the modification of gambling habits on different aspects of the client's life

Overview

At follow-ups, the therapist will check whether the client has maintained his or her objective. The therapist will also look for *DSM-IV* diagnosis criteria for pathological gambling using Section 5 of the Diagnostic

Interview for Pathological Gambling (DIPG) (see Appendix). The therapist will also collect information related to the gambling habits of the client via Section 6 of the DIPG (see Appendix), as well as the Gambling-Related Questions exercise and Perceived Self-Efficacy Questionnaire introduced during the pretreatment assessment.

The crucial question at follow-ups is whether the changes have been maintained over the months following the end of the treatment. We suggest keeping in touch with the client every 3 months for at least 1 year. Several clients have told us they find it very reassuring to know they won't be left on their own and will be contacted after the end of the treatment. Follow-up appointments reinforce the perception of self-efficacy for those who are doing well and help those who are drifting from their objectives or experiencing "slips" or relapses to get back on track.

Chapter 11

Difficulties Related to the Treatment

All therapists are well aware that clinical reality is more difficult or different than what one anticipates, and the treatment of pathological gambling is no exception. Some situations or behaviors can be disconcerting to the therapist. For example, what can be done if a gambler asserts that chance does not exist or that he is receiving threats from a loan shark? One thing is certain: the list of difficulties that can arise in therapy is infinite. In this chapter we present some of these difficulties and propose solutions.

There Is No Such Thing as Chance

The main component of treatment is based on a better understanding of chance. Gamblers misunderstand chance and often confuse games of chance with games of skill. As mentioned previously, the therapist and gambler must agree on a definition of chance. The majority of gamblers will define chance as an uncontrollable and unpredictable phenomenon. However, the therapist may sometimes meet gamblers who confidently assert that chance does not exist! What can be done with such a situation?

First, the therapist can ask these gamblers to explain what they mean exactly by this assertion. Some gamblers will assert that life is programmed in advance. They believe that chance is akin to destiny, everything is already planned, and one can do nothing to change the course or outcomes of events. Others will define chance from an even more philosophical point of view. According to these determinists, all events have a reason for being and everything happens for a reason. Some gamblers will also allude to premonitions, luck, and feelings. Others will defend the idea that chance is a probability and that one can predict events with clever calculations.

It is not advisable to confront such gamblers on their ideas about chance. However, it is still necessary to agree on a more down-to-earth definition of this concept. Any definition of chance must involve the notions of unpredictability and absence of control. Here is an example in which a therapist helps a gambler to accept and understand the definition used in therapy.

Case Vignette

Therapist: You're telling me that there is no such thing as chance. What exactly do you mean by that?

Gambler: What I mean is that I don't believe that the things that happen to us are by chance. You know, there are people who are luckier than others, people who have something special. It is not chance or an accident that some people win more often. There are people who can feel things. Things never happen for no reason.

Therapist: You seem to have thought about this question a lot and your view of chance is quite philosophical. What we mean here by chance in gambling games could be directly taken out of a dictionary. If I asked you to explain what chance is to a young child, what would be your explanation?

Gambler: I would say that it is something that happens and that we can't plan it. We can't know if it will happen or at what moment it will occur. And regardless of what we do, it will happen, it happens.

Therapist: So, chance is something that we can't plan, and on which our actions have no impact, since what must happen happens. Do you agree with this definition?

Gambler: Yes, it's pretty much that. It's quite a simple and narrow definition, but it can also be that.

This method of insisting on a dictionary definition has the advantage of not frustrating gamblers and often helps them to dissociate chance from notions of destiny, luck, and even premonitions. This approach does not involve denying that premonitions and destiny are part of some people's realities, but simply to spread doubt as to their efficacy when it comes to games of chance. Such an approach also avoids interminable discussions about the true definition of chance.

When gamblers refer to the idea of using clever and sophisticated mathematical strategies to predict chance events, the therapist can point out the major difference in how to cope with daily situations compared to the scientific expertise of an actuary in establishing insurance fees. Even if there were a machine that was able to calculate every probability, it could never predict the result of the next draw.

To sum up, because the proper course of treatment rests on a correct understanding of chance, it is very important that gamblers and therapists agree upon its definition. It is pointless to confront gamblers on their vision of chance. We may have to be satisfied with a mutually agreed upon, simple and operational definition of chance that is based on the fact that one can neither predict nor control it. While it is preferable that this understanding be reached at the beginning of therapy, this idea can occasionally be put aside and addressed later in the process.

Viewing Games of Chance as Games of Skill

Despite all the information and explanations that the therapist can provide gamblers regarding the uncontrollable and unpredictable nature of games of chance, some gamblers persist in viewing games of chance as games of skill.

It is now known that commercially exploited games of chance are chosen on the grounds of two very precise characteristics: (1) that it is impossible for a person to predict the result of the next game and (2) that no skill is required to play.

Unfortunately, stories still circulate that maintain false beliefs in the possibility to master certain games of chance. Many books and magazines exist that perpetuate these myths and maintain these illusions of control.

We believe it is essential to remain skeptical about these claims. Some may be true, while others are clearly mythical. It is quite possible that expelled gamblers, a very rare phenomenon, are part of an underground network working within casinos. The result is that gamblers cling to these stories and to the idea that there is a way to control chance. They wish to get the better of chance. They want to be the big winner!

Admittedly, while chance plays a large part in the outcome of many card games, a gambler's skill and experience effectively increase his or her chances of winning at certain card games. Bridge players, for example, use strategies and make deductions to better stand up against an opponent. And, when playing poker between friends, knowing how to bluff can be very useful. In this type of game, it is possible to improve and it is not misleading to believe in one's skill. Casinos are well aware of this reality, however, and do not take any risks. They systematically eliminate any kind of game where skill can make the results lean in favor of the gamblers.

Moreover, while games of chance and money offer no opportunity for financial return in the long run, nothing prevents gamblers from proceeding in a way that limits their losses. For example, in blackjack, the only skill required consists of obeying certain basic rules in order to lose less in the long run. But beyond obeying these rules, gamblers can in no way increase their chances of winning. Conversely, disobeying these rules results in an increase in the probabilities of losses over the long run.

In blackjack and other card games, gamblers often fantasize about eventually being able to count cards like "professional" gamblers who make their living thanks to this rare talent. This is a lovely myth. If we consider the reality imposed by a return rate that is less than 100%, it is absolutely impossible for a person who repeatedly plays to come out a winner. And although blackjack offers a very high return rate, approximately 99%, it still remains inferior to 100%.

Some gamblers claim that by counting cards, it becomes possible to increase their return, which would allow them to have an advantage over the casino. But this improvement in their return is not conceivable unless one plays with only one deck of cards. In casinos, three, five, or even six decks of cards are used within a single shoe, which is surely to the casino owner's advantage.

Let us take a look at the numbers. Consider a person who perfectly counts cards and who claims to have a 0.5% advantage over the casino. In the best of cases, if this person bets $100.00 each hand, he or she wins, on average, $0.05 per hand. Thus, if he or she plays 60 hands at $100.00 ($6,000.00), he or she will have won $30.00. What purpose does it serve to risk $6,000.00 for the possibility, not certainty, of winning $30.00? It's insane. Furthermore, these "professional gamblers" advise you to have 300 times your average bet in your pocket in order to face variations in potential losses. But the probabilities have been established over a long period of time. Gamblers could very well win their first two bets and then lose the next 20. This proves that even by counting cards, it is impossible to predict with certainty which card the dealer will turn up. Let us also add that at the beginning of a deck, the dealer asks a gambler to cut the shoe with a colored plastic card, which the dealer then uses to indicate the end of the shoe. Consequently, certain cards will never be revealed. How can one guess which cards? It is impossible. The structure of the game prevents anyone from winning in the long run. So, regardless of which strategy is used, the only law that prevails is the law of chance.

However, gamblers have difficulty admitting that they have no impact on the game's result. Over the years, they have often developed a great number of strategies that they believe will help them to play better and gain an advantage. This is a huge deception. Thus it is normal, even predictable, that many gamblers are depressed and self-deprecating when they learn this bad news. "How could I have been so stupid all these years?" they ask themselves. The therapist's job is to reassure them. The therapist can explain that, before therapy, the gambler did not know the traps of gambling games, so it was difficult for him or her to resist these traps, which are brilliantly orchestrated. Moreover, at that time, the gambler simply did not possess the knowledge needed to face them. The therapist can help discouraged gamblers see that it is not their lack of intelligence, but rather a lack of information, that greatly limited their freedom of choice.

This phenomenon repeats itself among horse race and sports betting amateurs. At the racetrack or in the betting parlor, one can find many "connoisseur" bettors who apparently have been tipped off and know the horses on which to bet. Nonetheless, research has demonstrated that an inexperienced bettor will lose as much as the most specialized bettor. The reason is simple: the rate of return at horse races is also less than 100%. Let us cite what is clearly specified in a racetrack's rules: "The race-track acts as a stock market firm, deducting a fixed percentage of the wagers made, regardless of the finish-line results. Winning bettors share the bets once the taxes and administration fees are deducted."

It should also be noted that the more often a horse is picked, the less return there is for a winning bet made on it. Moreover, the amount won after a race depends on the total sum of money that was bet by all bettors. Additionally, simple bets (one horse or one race) offer a smaller return than combined bets (two horses or more and several races). The same rule prevails for betting in other sports: the more probable the result, the smaller the win. Finally, who can predict whether a horse might trip and bring down its opponent, the horse we predicted would place first? It is impossible for anyone to know which horse will win. The same applies to other sports betting: how can one predict the injury or blunders of a star player?

In sum, there are so many parameters that determine the course of a race or sports game that it is absolutely impossible to predict the result. Only one thing is certain: the more a person bets, the more he or she loses.

Believing in the Idea of Control

We are still not able to say whether it is possible for a person with a pathological gambling problem to one day be able to gamble in a controlled fashion. However, we can assert without a doubt that one of the biggest illusions that gamblers can entertain is the belief that they can gamble "just $20," convincing themselves that they will be able to restrain themselves from gambling any more.

Gamblers must learn to admit that if they decide to play "only" $20, they greatly risk being swept away and spending a lot more. In fact, their experience has likely proven this to them several times. Eventually, they will come to understand that the idea of gambling only $20 is one of the justifications they invent to give themselves "permission" to gamble. They must beware of these dangerous ideas that make them lose control and push them to gamble again.

Case Vignette

Gambler: I told myself that I would just wager $20, calmly, and that I had the means to risk $20. I figured I could stop myself once the money was spent. I thought that it wouldn't do any harm.

Therapist: Let's write down what you said and look at each of these ideas. You said that you would just gamble $20, calmly. This idea encouraged you to gamble. With your experience as a gambler and the knowledge you have acquired up until now, what could you tell yourself in order to decrease your desire to gamble?

Gamblers: I could tell myself that I have never just wagered $20! That amount is so quickly spent! Also, I'm not able to gamble calmly. When I lose, I accelerate the rhythm and I don't relax at all. I become extremely stressed and I dive my hands back into my pockets to find more money to bet.

Therapist: Excellent! You should look reality in the face and beware of the idea that you can calmly gamble only $20, which has but one role: to encourage you to gamble again. You should modify this idea in order for it to go in the direction you wish: to not gamble. Let's now look at the second idea: "I have the means to risk $20 and I figured I could stop myself once it was spent."

Gambler: I could tell myself that I do not have the means to lose $20 because I know full well that if I'm going to gamble, I'll spend a lot more. That would be very harmful to me. If I do that, I won't have any money left at all to gamble with. I'm unable to control myself once I start gambling. I go crazy! So I'm telling myself lies when I tell myself that I'll be able to stop after having spent only $20.

Thanks to this kind of exercise, gamblers understand that they have the power to control their thoughts and actions, and that they can modify them. They become aware of the automatic thoughts that lead them to gamble, while learning at the same time how to modify them with the assistance of acquired knowledge and their willingness to stop gambling. If gamblers practice this type of exercise, they will become stronger and become masters of their destiny. When a risky situation presents itself, they will be better able to resist their desire to gamble.

Gambling Is Exciting

Some gamblers compare gambling to the consumption of drugs. Gambling provides them with excitement that no other activity can offer them. Some gamblers experience physical withdrawal sensations when they are craving or when it is impossible for them to gamble. Accordingly, these people suffer a lot when they stop their gambling activities.

When a person has a serious gambling problem, the state of excitement tends to decrease as he or she continue to gamble. This forces him or her to increase the "dose." Like the alcoholic or drug addict, gamblers progressively need to wager more and more in order to attain their desired degree of excitement.

Remembering the experience of powerful excitement is one of the thoughts that incite gamblers to gamble. The promise of strong sensations provides a good reason to gamble. Gamblers might also believe that nothing can produce the powerful sensations that gambling does and that only gambling allows them forget everything. Their thoughts tend to focus on the positive aspects of gambling rather than the negative consequences.

It is not necessary to directly attack the gambler's perception. However, the therapist can sow seeds of doubt in the gambler's mind. Asking gamblers to carefully observe themselves before and during gambling sessions is one very effective method. What is the intensity of their pleasure, and in what way does it vary over the course of the session? Gamblers will probably discover that they do not experience as much pleasure as they thought. The anticipated pleasure never equals the actual pleasure experienced when gambling. They will notice that they find gambling pleasurable only when they win. When they think about it, they may notice that they feel more relieved than triumphant when they win. This personal realization often carries more weight for gamblers than a therapist's observation.

Refusing to Change Thoughts

In general, when gamblers stubbornly maintain an idea, it is useless to convince them otherwise. Take the example of gamblers who are convinced that they will stop gambling once they have won "one last time." For the moment, they are always losing, but they firmly believe that they will cease gambling when they win. The therapist may try desperately to get them to see that even if they were to win, all of their false hopes would rise to the surface again and their sole desire would be to gamble more. However, the gambler is certain to stick to this idea for as long as he or she refuses to confront reality. The therapist can suggest to these gamblers that they make systematic observations or even take a break in treatment in order to test their hypothesis. Such an exercise wastes the time of neither the therapist nor the gambler and, in the future, can help them avoid discussions that lead nowhere.

It is also possible that gamblers will find the treatment simplistic and claim that their problem has deeper roots than the therapist thinks. In this case, it should be clearly reiterated that this therapy is interested in the factors that maintain gambling habits rather than their causes. It is necessary that people cease gambling before they can recover control of their lives. The example of a house on fire well illustrates this assertion.

Case Vignette

Therapist: I understand very well that your gambling problem has deep causes and that it's important for you to get to the source of the problem. However, I would nonetheless like to make a comparison. Your current situation resembles a house in flames. Everything is burning: the financial situation, family, work, the stress that's eating you up, etc.

Gambler: Yeah, it looks like that.

Therapist: What is the first thing to do in case of a fire?

Gambler: Leave the house as quickly as possible.

Therapist: And then?

Gambler: Call the fire department so that they'll put out the fire.

Therapist: Exactly. That's the most logical thing to do. The therapy that I'm offering here aims to help you get out of your house and put out the fire. Then we can explore the causes of the blaze. We can't explore the causes while the fire is burning. So I'm suggesting that we proceed by steps. The first step consists of working toward the cessation of gambling behavior, so that your life stops burning up. Then, you can take the time to explore causes and really get to the bottom of things. Does that proposition suit you? Think about it carefully and then make your decision.

With this attitude, we respect the gambler while explaining our way of conducting therapy. Moreover, we often notice that what perpetuates gambling behavior is not what triggered it. To slow the gambling problem, what maintains gambling habits must first be attacked. Erroneous ideas about gambling assuredly are the most important maintaining factor. Belief in the possibility of recouping losses, gambling only $20, relaxing by gambling, and forgetting problems are some of the many ideas that encourage people to gamble.

However, if the gambler still insists in finding in-depth and unconscious causes of his or her gambling problems, the therapist has two options. If he or she feels able to do it, the therapist can accompany the gambler in this process. If not, the therapist can refer the gambler to another therapist who works in this perspective.

Tardiness, Absences, and Missed Appointments

There are many reasons clients arrive late to their sessions, miss them entirely, or reschedule them. These behaviors often reflect the person's ambivalence regarding his or her decision to stop gambling.

Gamblers should be told that their reactions are normal. By warning gamblers of these possibilities, they will perhaps be less tempted to lie or to invent reasons to explain their absences or tardiness.

Table 11.1 Reasons for Missed Appointments

Lack of money	The gambler may not be able to pay for his session.
A relapse	The gambler may feel guilty toward his therapist. He may think he has betrayed the therapist's confidence and prefers to avoid the meeting. He may feel ashamed to admit his relapse.
Loss of confidence	A relapse erodes a gambler's self-confidence. As a result, he may believe he is unable to cease gambling and tell himself that it is not worth continuing therapy.
Doubt about the therapeutic process	A relapse can weaken belief in the benefits of therapy. A gambler may think that the therapy is ineffective because he relapsed.

Some reasons clients may have for rescheduling or canceling their appointments are shown in Table 11.1.

The therapist should come to an understanding with gamblers at the beginning of therapy. They should agree on what are acceptable and unacceptable excuses for being late or absent from appointments. Most importantly, the therapist should warn gamblers that lateness and absences are situations that are likely to occur and to agree on this issue.

Lying During Therapy

Lying is one of the diagnostic criteria for excessive gambling. It is an obvious symptom. Therapists can only work with the material that gamblers wish to share. Of course, the therapist might speak with the other people in the gambler's life with permission. However, a relationship must first develop between the gambler and the therapist. It is important to have an open attitude with gamblers and to avoid all forms of moralization. A condescending attitude could lead gamblers to hide certain things because they do not want the therapist to lecture them or to perceive them negatively.

Gamblers and their therapists form a team with a common goal: for the client to quit gambling. It is to the client's advantage to be frank with the therapist. The therapist may provide some examples of situations that may lead gamblers to lie over the course of therapy. Gamblers may lie:

- To minimize the seriousness of the gambling problem

- To please the therapist

- To make the therapist believe that the situation is improving

- Because they are tired of coming to therapy and saying they have gambled again

- Because it is embarrassing or frightening for them to admit having committed illegal acts

- Because it is embarrassing for them to say they spent 12 hours gambling on the same machine that devoured $900, especially after having reached the eighth session of therapy and they were aware of the game's traps

- Because they need to succeed in therapy, such as in the case of a court order

- To explain why they were late or absent from an appointment

The therapist can never be certain of the veracity of gamblers' assertions. Nonetheless, the therapist will use whatever elements gamblers wish to reveal and help them to the best of his or her ability.

Lack of Cooperation

Some clients say that they do not like filling out self-observation forms or that they do not have enough time to complete proposed homework assignments. Together with the therapist, the gambler will try to discover the reasons why he or she does not want to practice the required exercises—for instance, What do the exercises represent for him or her? What doesn't he or she like about the exercises? It is important to be creative while remaining focused on cognitions.

Depression and Suicidal Ideation

Obviously, if gamblers show severe signs of depression or suicidal thoughts, these problems should be treated as priorities. No risks should be taken with a person who is very depressed or suicidal. First, the therapist must ensure that the gambler knows to whom to turn or where to go to if intense suicidal ideas surface. The therapist can also make a life contract with the gambler. Depending on the situation, it might be appropriate to suggest that the gambler consult a doctor and to obtain medical or pharmacologic monitoring. It is essential to see to the gambler's safety. The therapist and gambler can return to therapy once the situation has stabilized.

Financial Issues

Two situations of financial trouble are when gamblers are being threatened by loan sharks and when gamblers are requesting financial aid from friends and/or family.

When gamblers are being threatened by loan sharks, they undoubtedly have very severe gambling problems. This is a particularly delicate situation, as gamblers often associate with the criminal element. In light of the very real dangers that gamblers face, we, as therapists, need to realize the limitations of our interventions.

Obviously, it is very difficult to conduct therapy under such conditions. Fear of reprisals becomes a motivation for gamblers to gamble. These threats perpetuate the problem because to reimburse the loan shark or bookie, gamblers must find money quickly, and the only way they know how to make money quickly is by gambling. Obviously, one cannot easily remove oneself from such a scene.

At this stage, gamblers should not have any access to money because the temptation to gamble will be too great. If they are in therapy, they should be closely monitored and a third person should manage their finances. If possible, an agreement with friends and family should be made to reimburse the loan shark. The therapist must be aware of the traumatic nature of this aspect of gamblers' experiences because their physical integrity, or that of friends and family, is being threatened. Such threats activate survival reflexes: fight or flight. Here we suggest some solutions that may be adopted according to the situation. Remember that gamblers who owe money to the criminal element find themselves in a serious situation, and it is possible that the therapist will be unable to assist them.

First, the therapist can suggest that gamblers treat the loan shark or bookie as a priority. Gamblers can choose to make an agreement with the "lender" or try to postpone the due date of their repayments. It may be preferable for the loan shark to wait longer in order to get back what is owed rather than physically harm the gambler and never recoup the money. Even if gamblers file for bankruptcy, they cannot escape their debt when the lender isn't "legal."

Like victims of domestic violence, gamblers who are being threatened by a loan shark might consider escape. However, there are no "safe houses" for gamblers. Moving or running away may be a safe solution in the short term, but it does not guarantee safety in the medium or long term. Gamblers might decide instead to reimburse the "lender" and to assume the consequences. Fortunately, cases where gamblers are indebted to someone dangerous are relatively rare.

Often, gamblers' friends or family contact the therapist in order to know whether they should lend them money. Important financial difficulties frequently push gamblers to ask friends and family to lend them money. Friends and family find themselves in difficult, even heartrending situations because they want to help the gambler to recover, but at the same time they do not know whether lending them money is the right thing to do. Furthermore, they know very well that it is very unlikely that gamblers will be able to repay them.

The therapist can provide advice to friends and family, but the decision of whether or not to lend the gambler money is entirely theirs. The therapist's role is to inform these people of the possible consequences of lending money, not to decide for them.

We generally advise friends and family not to lend money to the gambler. If he or she has not yet taken responsibility for the financial consequences of gambling, borrowing money is likely to minimize them. Gamblers might even decide to continue gambling if they are being lent money. We know that it is difficult for friends and family to refuse lending money because of their emotional connection and also because gamblers are often masters in the arts of manipulation and lying. And even if gamblers truly have every intention of returning the money they borrow, their problem will drive them to gamble, even if they win. Friends and family might be afraid that the gambler will be driven to suicide if he or she does not overcome his or her financial difficulties.

Despite all, it is in the interest of the gambler's friends and family to protect themselves financially and to ensure that the gambler does not lead them into a financial abyss. To do so, friends and family might ask a financial counselor, notary, or lawyer to assist them. Unless they have a limitless source of money, nobody can finance the practice of pathological gambling because losing money is the only possible consequence of excessive gambling.

Stagnation of Treatment

If therapy seems to plateau or to be going in circles, it is time to stop and analyze the situation. The therapist should first determine whether the client has the same impression and then ask him or her if he or she can explain the stagnation. Several questions may be asked to assess the situation: What progress has been made since the beginning of therapy? Do certain aspects of the therapy displease the gambler? Does he or she understand the concepts addressed? Is he or she able to apply the new strategies? The therapist can also question the gambler's ambivalence, review his or her therapeutic goals, and identify other activities that would help him or her stay away from gambling.

Ignorance of the Game the Gambler Plays

There are many different games of chance, including card games, lottery, sports betting, slot machines, and video lotteries. Consequently, the therapist may not know very much about the game the gambler plays. What can be done in this case? The therapist can simply admit to having limited knowledge of this game and say that he or she would like to know more about its rules, the way it is played, the possible wins, and so forth. For the therapist, this is a great occasion to explore the gambler's erroneous cognitions about his or her favorite game. It is not necessary to know the particular game well to be able to detect erroneous perceptions; it is enough to be attentive to the gambler's conviction of winning, illusions of control, and tendency to make links between independent events. The therapist can thus kill two birds with one stone: he or she will learn about the game being discussed and will have the opportunity to work on the gambler's many errors in thinking related to the particular game.

Conclusion

We have presented some thoughts on the difficulties that can occur during therapy. Based on our experience, we have suggested some solutions that may be useful in dealing with these difficulties. These clues might serve as a starting point on your search for solutions to therapeutic difficulties. We would like to end here by saying that it is better to bet on our strengths than on chance.

Appendix | *Diagnostic Interview on Pathological Gambling*

Section 1: Motive of Consultation

Section 2: Games That Lead to a Partial or Complete Loss of Control

Section 3: Information on the Development of Gambling Habits

Section 4: Information on Current Gambling Problem

Section 5: DSM-IV Diagnostic Criteria

Section 6: Consequences of the Gambling Problem

Section 7: Suicidal Ideation

Section 8: Current Living Conditions

Section 9: Other Dependencies (Present or Past)

Section 10: Mental Health—Prior Experiences

Section 11: Strengths and Available Resources

Section 12: Comments

Date _____ / _____ / _____
       Month   Day   Year

Participant _____

Therapist _____

SECTION 1: MOTIVE OF CONSULTATION

1. What aspects of your gambling have led you to consult with us?

_____

_____

_____

2. Are you *personally* motivated to undertake measures to resolve your gambling?

Yes ☐   No ☐

Explain: _____

_____

_____

3. Is there a particular event that motivated you to seek help?

Do not read choice of answers. You can probe to find up to three reasons (first reason = 1, second reason = 2, third reason = 3)

Yes ☐   No ☐

		Comments
Threat of separation or pressure from spouse because of gambling	_____	_____
Loss of a relationship because of gambling	_____	_____
Threats or pressure from employer	_____	_____
Loss of employment due to gambling	_____	_____
Loss of control over gambling activities	_____	_____
Loss of significant possessions	_____	_____
Other (explain):	_____	_____

SECTION 2: GAMES THAT LEAD TO A PARTIAL OR COMPLETE LOSS OF CONTROL

	Do you have difficulty controlling yourself at this game? (Yes / No)	If yes, how long have you had this difficulty? (Number of months or years)
A. Lotteries		
B. Casino		
Blackjack		
Roulette		
Baccarat		
Keno		
Slot Machines		
C. Bingo		
D. Cards		
E. Horse, dog, or other types of animal racing		
F. Stock market or commodities		
G. Video lottery terminals (VLT)		
H. Bowling, pool, golf, or other skill games		
I. Dice (craps, etc.)		
J. Sports wagering		
K. Internet wagering		
L. Others		

Comments:

_____

_____

_____

_____

SECTION 3: INFORMATION ON THE DEVELOPMENT OF GAMBLING HABITS

1. You have told me that you experienced difficulty in the past controlling your gambling, when playing certain games of chance for money. When you first played these games, do you remember having had a significant win, i.e., having "won big"?

NB: large wins within the first few experiences with the game(s) in question qualify as a "YES" in this instance.

Yes ☐   No ☐

If yes, how much did you win? _____

What was the amount of your bet? _____

How long ago was this? _____
(Specify in months or years)

2. Which of the following people introduced you to gambling (specify the relationship)?

Father	☐	Spouse	☐
Mother	☐	Friend	☐
Brother/Sister	☐	Neighbor	☐
Aunt/Uncle	☐	Work colleague	☐
Grandfather/Grandmother	☐	Myself	☐
Other (Specify) _____ ☐			

3. How old were you when gambling became a problem for you? _____

4. In your opinion, what triggered your gambling problem? _____

_____

_____

_____

_____

_____

SECTION 4: INFORMATION ON CURRENT GAMBLING PROBLEM

1. What are the main reasons or issues that motivate you to gamble at this point?

   To distract yourself, change your ideas or escape daily problems and stresses ☐

   To make money or resolve a financial problem ☐

   Other reason(s): ☐

2. On average, how much time do you spend gambling each week? _____ (total hours)

3. On average, how much money do you spend gambling in one week? $_____

You must read each item as described below. If after reading the questions below as stated and the individual does not understand, then you may reformulate the question to improve understanding. For each of the *DSM-IV* criteria, you must be able to clearly state YES or NO whether the individual meets each criteria. If doubt remains, probing might be necessary.

1. Do you find that you are preoccupied with gambling (for example, preoccupied with reliving past gambling experiences, handicapping or planning the next venture, or thinking of ways to get money with which to gamble)?

    Yes ☐   No ☐

2. Do you need to gamble with increasing amounts of money in order to achieve the desired excitement?

    Yes ☐   No ☐

    2a. If yes, do you have the tendency to increase your bet or do you always bet the maximum amount?

    Yes ☐   No ☐

3. Have you already made repeated unsuccessful efforts to control, cut back, or stop gambling?

    Yes ☐   No ☐

    If yes, comment: _____

    _____

    _____

4. Have you felt restless or irritable when attempting to cut down or stop gambling?

    Yes ☐   No ☐

5. Do you gamble in order to escape from problems or to relieve a dysphoric mood (e.g., feelings of helplessness, guilt, anxiety, or depression)?

    Yes ☐   No ☐

6. After losing money gambling, do you often return on another occasion to "break even" ("chase one's losses")?

    Yes ☐   No ☐

7. Has it happened that you have lied to your family members, therapist, or others to conceal the extent of your involvement in gambling?

    Yes ☐   No ☐

8. Have you committed illegal acts such as forgery, fraud, theft, or embezzlement to finance gambling?

Yes ☐   No ☐

8a. If yes, which illegal acts and how many times?

		Number of times
False check	☐	_____
Fraud	☐	_____
Theft	☐	_____
Embezzlement	☐	_____
Other (Specify) _____	☐	_____

8b. Do you currently have legal problems or are you in the middle of legal proceedings? If yes, explain:

_____

_____

9. Have you jeopardized or lost a significant relationship, job, or educational opportunity because of gambling?

Yes ☐   No ☐

If yes, did they involve....?

Family relations	☐	Work	☐
Spousal Relations	☐	Friendships	☐
Work relationships	☐	Studies	☐

Explain: _____

_____

_____

10. Do you rely on others to provide you with money to relieve desperate financial situations caused by gambling?

Yes ☐   No ☐

NUMBER OF DIAGNOSTIC CRITERIA PRESENT:

SECTION 6: CONSEQUENCES OF THE GAMBLING PROBLEM

1. At present, to what point does your gambling behavior affect your *social life* (reduction of the number of friends, isolation, abandoning social activities, etc.)?

```
0---------------1---------------2---------------3---------------4---------------5-------------NA
```
Not at all   Very little   Somewhat   Moderately   Much   A great deal
No problem   Severe
                                                           problems

Explain: _____

_____

2. At present, to what point does your gambling behavior affect your *marital life* (arguments, decrease in time spent with partner, irritability, frequency of sexual activities, etc.)

```
0---------------1---------------2---------------3---------------4---------------5-------------NA
```
Not at all   Very little   Somewhat   Moderately   Much   A great deal
No problem   Severe
                                                           problems

Explain: _____

_____

3. At present, to what point does your gambling behavior affect your *family life* (absences, decrease in time spent with children, irritability, etc.)?

```
0---------------1---------------2---------------3---------------4---------------5-------------NA
```
Not at all   Very little   Somewhat   Moderately   Much   A great deal
No problem   Severe
                                                           problems

Explain: _____

_____

4. At present, to what point does your gambling behavior affect your *work* (decrease in efficiency, absences, lateness, lack of concentration, etc.)?

```
0---------------1---------------2---------------3---------------4---------------5-------------NA
```
Not at all   Very little   Somewhat   Moderately   Much   A great deal
No problem   Severe
                                                            problems

Explain: _____

_____

5. At present, to what point does your gambling behavior affect your *mood* (anxiety, worries, stress, depression, etc.)?

0---------------1 ---------------2 ---------------3 ---------------4---------------5 ------------NA

Not at all   Very little   Somewhat   Moderately   Much   A great deal
No problem   Severe
                                                                              problems

Explain: _____

6. At present, to what point does your gambling behavior affect your *sleep* (difficulty falling asleep or staying asleep, waking up too early in the morning, etc.)?

0---------------1 ---------------2 ---------------3 ---------------4---------------5 ------------NA

Not at all   Very little   Somewhat   Moderately   Much   A great deal
No problem   Severe
                                                                              problems

Explain: _____

7. At present, to what point does your gambling behavior affect your *physical health* (weight loss, stomach ulcers, headaches, etc.)?

0---------------1 ---------------2 ---------------3 ---------------4---------------5 ------------NA

Not at all   Very little   Somewhat   Moderately   Much   A great deal
No problem   Severe
                                                                              problems

Explain: _____

8. At present, to what point does your gambling behavior affect your *financial situation*?

0---------------1 ---------------2 ---------------3 ---------------4---------------5 ------------NA

Not at all   Very little   Somewhat   Moderately   Much   A great deal
No problem   Severe
                                                                              problems

Explain: _____

continued

8a. Have you ever declared bankruptcy?

　　　Yes ☐　　No ☐

　　　If yes, when? ＿＿＿＿＿＿ (*indicate the year*)

　　　What was the amount of the debt?　$＿＿＿＿＿

　　　What amount was directly related to gambling?　$＿＿＿＿＿

8b. At present, do you have gambling debts?

　　　Yes ☐　　No ☐

　　　If yes, to whom do you owe money?

Bank/Credit Union	＿＿＿＿＿	Amount owed $＿＿＿＿＿
Partner	＿＿＿＿＿	Amount owed $＿＿＿＿＿
Relative	＿＿＿＿＿	Amount owed $＿＿＿＿＿
Friend	＿＿＿＿＿	Amount owed $＿＿＿＿＿
Colleague	＿＿＿＿＿	Amount owed $＿＿＿＿＿
Loan shark	＿＿＿＿＿	Amount owed $＿＿＿＿＿
Other	＿＿＿＿＿	Amount owed $＿＿＿＿＿

8c. What do you estimate is the total amount of money lost as a result of gambling up to today?

　　　$＿＿＿＿＿

9. At present, to what point does your gambling behavior affect your *quality of life* (housing, diet, purchases of personal possession, personal care, etc.)?

```
o--------------I---------------2---------------3---------------4---------------5------------NA
```

Not at all No problem	Very little	Somewhat	Moderately	Much	A great deal Severe problems

Explain: ＿＿＿＿＿＿＿＿＿＿＿＿＿＿＿＿＿＿＿＿＿＿＿＿＿＿＿＿＿＿

＿＿＿＿＿＿＿＿＿＿＿＿＿＿＿＿＿＿＿＿＿＿＿＿＿＿＿＿＿＿＿＿＿＿

SECTION 7: PRESENCE OF SUICIDAL IDEATION

1. In the past 12 months, have you ever SERIOUSLY thought about committing suicide (putting an end to your life)?

   Yes ☐   No ☐

   1.b. If YES, had you thought about a way to do it?

   Yes ☐   No ☐

   1.c. Was this thought mainly linked to your gambling problems?

   Yes ☐   No ☐

   1.d. Did you ever attempt suicide (tried to end your life) in the last 12 months?

   Yes ☐   No ☐

2. Have you ever attempted suicide?

   Yes ☐   No ☐

   2.b. IF YES, in what year? _____

   2.c. Explain the context:

   _____

   _____

   _____

   _____

3. Are you presently considering suicide?

   Yes ☐   No ☐

Comments:

_____

_____

_____

_____

_____

SECTION 8: CURRENT LIVING CONDITIONS

1. Describe your current lifestyle (living conditions, diet, close relationships, work, hobbies and leisure activities). (*Try to get an idea of the conditions and quality of the client's daily life in this section*)

_____

_____

_____

_____

_____

_____

_____

_____

_____

2. Do you use community services for food, clothing or other essential needs for yourself or your family? If yes, explain.

_____

_____

_____

_____

_____

_____

_____

_____

_____

_____

_____

SECTION 9: OTHER DEPENDENCIES (CURRENT AND PAST)

1. Do you currently or have you in the past had problems with the following behaviors:

	In the past?	Currently?	If yes, how did you resolve them?
Your cigarette smoking?	Yes ☐ No ☐	Yes ☐ No ☐	_____
Your drug use?	Yes ☐ No ☐	Yes ☐ No ☐	_____
Your alcohol use?	Yes ☐ No ☐	Yes ☐ No ☐	_____
Your medication use?	Yes ☐ No ☐	Yes ☐ No ☐	_____
Time spent on the Internet?	Yes ☐ No ☐	Yes ☐ No ☐	_____
Your sexual behavior?	Yes ☐ No ☐	Yes ☐ No ☐	_____
Your frequency of buying goods (compulsive buying)?	Yes ☐ No ☐	Yes ☐ No ☐	_____
Are there other behaviors?	Yes ☐ No ☐	Yes ☐ No ☐	_____

(Specify: _____)

For all dependency problems, please specify the nature of the problem (e.g., what type of drug? when did the problem start? etc.)

_____

_____

_____

_____

_____

_____

_____

_____

_____

continued

119

In relation to alcohol consumption…

2a. Do you drink before gambling?

Yes ☐   No ☐

If yes, what proportion of the time does this happen (e.g., 1/10; report %) _____

2b. Do you drink while you gamble?

Yes ☐   No ☐

If yes, what proportion of the time does this happen (e.g., 1/10; report %) _____

2c. Do you drink after you gamble?

Yes ☐   No ☐

If yes, what proportion of the time does this happen (e.g., 1/10; report %) _____

In relation to drug consumption…

3a. Do you use drugs before gambling?

Yes ☐   No ☐

If yes, what proportion of the time does this happen (e.g., 1/10; report %) _____

3b. Do you use drugs while you gamble?

Yes ☐   No ☐

If yes, what proportion of the time does this happen (e.g., 1/10; report %) _____

3c. Do you use drugs after you gamble?

Yes ☐   No ☐

If yes, what proportion of the time does this happen (e.g., 1/10; report %) _____

SECTION 10: PRESENCE OF PRIOR MENTAL HEALTH PROBLEMS

1. Have you ever consulted a doctor, psychologist, psychiatrist for other psychological difficulties?

     Yes ☐   No ☐

If yes…

What type of specialist?	When?	For what reason?

2. Are you currently taking prescribed medication?

     Yes ☐   No ☐

If yes…

Which medication?	For how long?	For what reason?

SECTION 11: PERSONAL STRENGHTS AND RESOURCES AVAILABLE

Discuss with the gambler in order to verify if he...

• Benefits from support from close ones, contacts, employer, etc.

_____

_____

_____

_____

_____

_____

_____

_____

_____

• Shows interest in other activities (leisure activities, hobbies, sports) other than gambling.

_____

_____

_____

_____

_____

_____

_____

_____

_____

_____

SECTION 12: COMMENTS

References

American Psychiatric Association (1994). *Diagnostic and statistical manual of mental disorders* (4th ed.). Washington DC: American Psychiatric Association.

Beaudoin, C., & Cox, B. (1999). Characteristics of problem gambling in a Canadian context: a preliminary study using a DSM-IV-based questionnaire. *Canadian Journal of Psychiatry, 44,* 483–487.

Beconia, E. (1992). Prevalence surveys of problem and pathological gambling in Europe: the cases of Germany, Holland and Spain. *Journal of Gambling Studies, 12,* 179–192.

Blaszczynski, A., & McConaghy, N. (1993). A two- to nine-year follow-up study of pathological gambling. In W. Eadington (Ed.), *Gambling behavior and problem gambling.* Institute for the Study of Gambling and Commercial Gaming, University of Nevada, Reno.

Blaszczynski, A., McConaghy, N., & Frankova, A. (1991). Control versus abstinence in the treatment of pathological gambling: a two- to nine-year follow-up. *British Journal of Addictions, 86,* 299–306.

Crockford, D. N., & el-Guebaly, N. (1998). Psychiatric comorbidity in pathological gambling: a critical review. *Canadian Journal of Psychiatry, 43,* 43–50.

Ladouceur, R. (1996). The prevalence of pathological gambling in Canada. *Journal of Gambling Studies, 12,* 129–142.

Ladouceur, R. (2004). Perceptions among pathological and non-pathological gamblers. *Addictive Behaviors, 29,* 555–565.

Ladouceur, R., Jacques, C., Chevalier, S., Sévigny, S., & Hamel, D. (2005). Prevalence of pathological gambling in Quebec in 2002. *Canadian Journal of Psychiatry, 50,* 451–456.

Ladouceur, R., Sylvain, C., Boutin, C., & Doucet, C. (2000). *Le jeu excessif: comprendre et vaincre le gambling.* Montréal: Les Éditions de l'Homme.

Ladouceur, R., Sylvain, C., Boutin, C., & Doucet, C. (2002). *Understanding and treating pathological gamblers.* London: Wiley.

Ladouceur, R., Sylvain, C., Boutin, C., Lachance, S., Doucet, C., Leblond, J., & Jacques, C. (2001). Cognitive treatment of pathological gambling. *Journal of Nervous and Mental Disease, 189*, 766–773.

Lejoyeux, M., Feuche, L., Loi, S., Solomon, J., & Ades, J. (1999). Study of impulsive control among alcohol-dependent patients. *Journal of Clinical Psychiatry, 60*, 302–305.

Linden, R. D., Pope, H. G., & Jonas, J. M. (1986). Pathological gambling and major affective disorder: preliminary findings. *Journal of Clinical Psychiatry, 47*, 201–203.

Marlatt, G. A., & Gordon, J. R. (Ed.). (1985). *Relapse prevention: maintenance strategies in the treatment of addictive behaviors.* New York: Guilford Press.

McCormick, R. A., Russo, A. M., Ramirez, L. F., & Taber, J. I. (1984). Affective disorders among pathological gamblers seeking treatment. *American Journal of Psychiatry, 141*, 215–218.

Miller, W. R. (1983). Motivational interviewing with problem drinkers. *Behavioural Psychotherapy, 11*, 147–172.

Miller, W. R., Benefield, R. G., & Tonigan, J. S. (1993). Enhancing motivation for change in problem drinking: a controlled comparison of two therapist styles. *Journal of Consulting and Clinical Psychology, 61*, 455–461.

Miller, W. R., & Rollnick, S. (1991). *Motivational interviewing: preparing people to change addictive behavior.* New York: Guilford Press.

Najavits, L. M. (2003). How to design an effective treatment outcome study. *Journal of Gambling Studies, 19*, 278–337.

National Gambling Impact Study Commission (1999). *Final report.* Washington DC: Government Printing Office.

Shaffer, H. J., Hall, M. N., & VanderBilt, J. (1997). Estimating the prevalence of disordered gambling behavior in the United States and Canada: a research synthesis. *American Journal of Public Health, 89*, 1369–1376.

Smart, R. G., & Ferris, J. (1996). Alcohol, drugs and gambling in the Ontario adult population. *Canadian Journal of Psychiatry, 41*, 36–45.

Sylvain, C., Ladouceur, R., & Boisvert, J.-M. (1997). Cognitive and behavioral treatment of pathological gambling: a controlled study. *Journal of Consulting and Clinical Psychology, 65*, 727–732.

Toneatto, T., & Ladouceur, R. (2003). The treatment of pathological gambling: a critical review of the literature. *Psychology of Addictive Behaviors, 17*, 284–292.

About the Authors

Robert Ladouceur is full professor in psychology at Laval University, Quebec, Canada, and a licensed clinical psychologist in the Province of Quebec. He is also the director of the Centre d'excellence pour la prevention et le traitement du jeu, a group of 20 researchers and clinicians working on different issues related to gambling (epidemiology, prevention, treatment, and the fundamental aspects of gambling behavior). He has published over 150 articles and chapters in the areas of gambling. His work on gambling is internationally known. He was invited twice to present his work at the National Gambling Impact Study Commission, the U.S. Presidential Commission on Gambling. In 1996, he received the Research Award from the National Council on Problem Gambling, recognizing the high quality of his work. In 2003, he received the Senior Research Award from the National Center for Responsible Gaming, Harvard University.

He has presented his work in many Canadian provinces, American states, and European and Asian countries. His cognitive treatment for pathological gamblers developed at Laval University is widely used. He recently published a paper on responsible gambling called the Reno Model with Alex Blaszczynski from the University of Sydney, Australia, and Howard Shaffer from Harvard University.

Stella Lachance is a psychologist who has worked at the Center of Excellence for the Prevention and Treatment of Problem Gambling at Laval University since 1996. As a clinician-researcher, she has been extensively involved in the development and delivery of treatment for pathological gambling and has provided therapy to many gamblers over the years. In addition, she contributed to the development of a step-by-step treatment guide for problem gamblers, which has been endorsed by the Quebec Ministry of Health and Social Services and is used by most treatment centers in the Province of Quebec. Since 2000, she has conducted many workshops, presented at conferences, and provided numerous training sessions on the treatment of problem gambling.